BEING A THERAPIST

BEING A THERAPIST
A Practitioner's Handbook

Mavis Klein

Routledge
Taylor & Francis Group

LONDON AND NEW YORK

First published 2012 by Karnac Books Ltd.

Published 2018 by Routledge
2 Park Square, Milton Park, Abingdon, Oxon OX14 4RN
711 Third Avenue, New York, NY 10017, USA

*Routledge is an imprint of the Taylor & Francis Group,
an informa business*

British Library Cataloguing in Publication Data

A C.I.P. for this book is available from the British Library

ISBN-13: 9781780490199 (pbk)

Typeset by Vikatan Publishing Solutions (P) Ltd., Chennai,
India

This book is dedicated with gratitude to the many people who have trusted me with their realities and have so enabled me to enlarge my own

CONTENTS

ABOUT THE AUTHOR

Mavis Klein has been a psychotherapist for the past thirty-five years. She is a founder member of the Institute of Transactional Analysis and of the European Association for Transactional Analysis. She is a team-building consultant to many organisations and businesses both in the UK and overseas, and gives lectures and conducts training workshops for executives. She is the author of eight previous books on psychological topics. She is also a qualified astrologer.

INTRODUCTION

There are as many kinds of psychotherapy as there are therapists. From a client's point of view, one therapy or therapist may be greatly different from another; but from a therapist's point of view, there is much that he or she has in common with all other therapists. This book is about being a therapist from the therapist's point of view.

Mind and body are increasingly understood to be a unity, and there are many therapies today that address our psychological as well as our bodily diseases through physical means. Nevertheless, in this book my presumption is that the therapist/counsellor is offering healing essentially through a verbal exchange, and my observations will be within that frame of reference, although I am confident that even the most physically oriented therapist will also find many of the ideas in this book relevant to his or her practice.

In writing this book, I have especially wanted to encourage advanced students and beginner practitioners to be confidently themselves in their interactions with their clients, notwithstanding all the rules and regulations that beset them and all the academic input they have received, which can seem so abstract and sterile in the reality of a face-to-face encounter with a human being in distress.

In a world where, increasingly, "the customer is always right" and professionals of all kinds are made to account for and justify their authority, I feel there is a crying need to redress the balance in a treatise that emphasises the wellbeing of the practitioner rather than the client. To this extent, I hope this book will also hearten experienced practitioners who are fed up and demoralised by the politically correct, bureaucratised constraints that so confine them today.

This book is non-academic and virtually jargon free; it is personal and anecdotal. It discriminates clearly between the responsibilities, cognitive understanding, and the feelings of the practitioner, and it is intended to be useful to all "humanistic" therapists and counsellors irrespective of their particular theoretical orientation.

Zeitgeist elaborates the existential issues that beset all human beings in contemporary Western society. Irrespective of the personal problems that our clients seek our help in overcoming, we share with them the pervasive stresses of post-modernism, which is the context that affects the particularities of all our lives. We and our clients benefit from sharing our awareness of the issues that we grapple with collectively.

Believing is about professionalism in its responsibilities and privileges. I hope this chapter in particular will support the reader in the expression of his or her self-confident authority in his or her relationship to his or her clients, which is the single most important characteristic that distinguishes the effectively potent therapist.

Thinking is about the substantive knowledge that enables the therapist to do the job of helping the client to solve his or her problems. It analyses the assumptions that underlie all humanistic theories and therapies and the samenesses and differences between individuals that need to inform the dialogues we have with our clients.

Five personality types is an outline of my own original theory of psychological health and pathology, developed inductively over twenty-five years of my clinical practice. It is in no way meant to compete with readers' own confidently established theoretical frames of reference, but I hope it will nonetheless be of interest and possibly provide an extra string to the bow of the practitioner.

Feeling is about the emotional satisfactions and tribulations associated with being a therapist. It is intended to encourage the reader to a shame-free understanding of his or her own hang-ups and the value they have in the joyfully creative work of being a therapist.

Implicitly, if not explicitly, the profession of psychotherapy is deeply philosophical, dealing as it does with "human nature". So I ask for the reader's indulgence, in the name of rational comprehensiveness, before beginning my main theme, to make explicit the chief timeless issues that underpin all our theories and practice.

Whether or not there has been or can be progress in matters pertaining to human nature is debatable. Civilisation is the usual name given to the structures of society that aim to increase the average overall happiness of the world. But these structures seem to be eminently fragile. Regular episodic outbursts of collective, uncivilised aggression seem to increase the average overall pain in the world in exact proportion to the degree of civilisation that is the current ideal. It is arguable that the sum total of pleasure and pain in the world must, because of the immutability of human nature, remain constant. As sons and daughters of Adam and Eve, we are all exiles from Paradise.

First and foremost, we are determined by our species' biology. Anthropology rules psychology which rules society and culture. Our consciousness of the imperfection of our human nature and our valiant struggles to perfect ourselves set us apart from all other species and has amongst its spin-offs all of art, science, and philosophy.

The bottom line of human consciousness is our awareness of our mortality. Reduced to its essence, human life is a desperate bid to deny or to find compensation for the fact that we must die. To this extent, we live most authentically and contentedly when we are explicitly fighting for our survival. But with full stomachs and in peace-time, we need to find causes and problems that serve as displacements of our basic quest for physical survival. Struggling, fighting, and succeeding in overcoming our quotidian problems distracts us from facing our mortality head on.

We never fully come to terms with the meaninglessness that death makes of our mundane concerns. Some people deny death by a belief in some form of eternal afterlife, others seek continuation of their lives after physical death through being remembered for their works or deeds, and most of us find some comfort in the knowledge of the survival of some of our genes in our children, grandchildren, and further descendants. But, one way or another, contentment in the face of our mortality is contingent on our living life as if it has meaning, even if it doesn't.

We make sense and meaning of life by concepts and categories into which we sort our experiences. First and foremost, we seek the meaning of pain. Universally, this quest creates in our minds the concept of "good and evil", with its inevitable moral derivatives of blame and responsibility, righteousness and guilt. Maturely, we are able appropriately to experience responsibility and guilt as well as righteousness and blame, although, being human—unless we are neurotically self-abnegating and masochistic—our first impulse is to find the cause of our own pains in somebody or something else.

Our hard-wired necessity to project blame for our pains was made vivid to me by one of my granddaughters. Then aged just two, she dropped and broke a cup in front of me. Despite my non-punitive, "Never mind" response, she compulsively expressed the most primitive of our ego's defences, denial, with, "I didn't, I didn't …". A few months later, considerably more sophisticated, while sitting opposite me at the kitchen table, she accidentally dropped some food on the floor, stared straight at me, and declared, "I think you did that"!

Physically and psychologically, our completed selves are products of nature and nurture. Nurture has its say— witness the increased height of recent generations and our increased longevity due to improved nutrition and hygiene—but nature is dominant and is now precisely mapped. So how can we justify the deeply embedded Freudian presumption of all humanistic psychotherapies that we are born a *tabula rasa* on which are etched our personalities and characters through our earliest experiences?

My own resolution of this problem is that our earliest remembered experiences are *as if* causes of what we become. That is, our remembered childhood experiences, which our literary tradition and, latterly, psychoanalysis call the causes of our completed selves are actually selectively remembered by us to concur with our preordained genetic predispositions. Witness the often widely divergent memories and/or interpretations of shared experiences of siblings. But it doesn't matter that the environmental events of our early years are not "really" causes but are subsumed to the deeper determinism of our genes which, in turn, may be subsumed to an even deeper cause, to *karma* or whatever ... until we stop and call the "final cause" God—or Unified Field Theory. Our perceived causes of our pains are the outcome of our natural need to project blame, to which we are entitled, with the proviso that, healthily, we equally attend to the other side of the coin of our chosen currency, our own responsibility and guilt. Logically, we have two choices: either we "can't help" what we are because of what our parents did to us and they, in turn, couldn't help being as they were to us because of what was done to them ... to the original wrongdoing in the Garden of Eden; *or* our parents are blameworthy for what they did to us as we are blameworthy to our children for what we did to them, and so on through the generations. The no-blame option implies no praise either; the reciprocity of both blame and praise seems to be a universal and unavoidable construct of the human mind.

The corollary to this pragmatic conclusion is that, notwithstanding the overwhelming power of our genetic determinism, we do have free will, which is contained in the responses we choose to make to our own natures and to what befalls us. Our responses are our choices and these have consequences. We cannot avoid making choices. Passivity is the self-delusion of "no choice", but of course it is a choice and, like all others, has consequences. Psychotherapists are more aware than most other people that every moment of choice is the cause of the inexorable train of events that follows in its wake, to the natural conclusion of a "happening" in our lives. When a conclusion is painful, we are loath to remember the moment of choice that determined it, although repression is never complete, and often the knowledge that we have chosen a path to pain is manifest as obsessive fear of that pain—too late—and a conscious struggle to avoid it. We actually do know (in our hearts) that we have made the choices we have that have led to their inevitable conclusions. In our most intense moments, we are reduced to knowing, in all its simplicity, that in virtually—if not absolutely—everything that befalls us, we get exactly what we set out to get, and so what we deserve. However constrained we are by the genetic hand we have been dealt and its complicit endorsement by our earliest childhood memories, our free will is exercised on the long continuum between making the most and the best or the least and the worst of that hand.

While not often explicitly stated, psychoanalysis and its post-Freudian derivatives (which constitute the vast majority of contemporary humanistic psychotherapeutic frameworks) are concerned specifically with ego development—the growth of self-esteem. Jungian analysis and other transpersonal therapies are exceptional in addressing more holistically our ultimate spiritual quest for meaning, which refers to the transcendence of the ego in favour of a return to oneness with the universe, which, it may be inferred, was the state in which we began our lives and, ideally, in the fullness of time, to which we return. But nobody has yet transcended their ego without having an ego to transcend, and the worthwhile work of most psychotherapy is about helping people find realistic ego satisfaction in their loving relationships and in their work, which is what (insistently atheistic) Freud argued is as much as we can hope and ask for of life.

The existential position of any human being at any time is informed by his or her age, individuality, and humanity. And our responses to another as "helpers" of that other, are informed by our awareness of our boundaries (moral code), theories (objective knowledge), and empathy (feelings). These three categories of our responses are consonant with the *ego states* of Transactional Analysis, which is my *lingua franca* as a psychotherapist. While I am myself enamoured of Transactional Analysis, I have no wish to impose it on my readers; but I ask leave to use a few words of the vocabulary of TA in the interest of concision, words I believe will not compromise the differing theoretical orientations of my readers. For the benefit of those readers unfamiliar with the basic vocabulary of TA, here are the few words and their meanings that I will interpolate where appropriate in my overall exposition.

The *ego states*, Parent, Adult, and Child (always capitalised), are the existential states of being into which our ego is divided. *Structurally*, our Parent contains our taught beliefs, values, and generalisations about life and the world; our Adult contains our skills and objective knowledge; and our Child contains our feelings, both innate and conditioned. *Functionally*, our Parent controls and nurtures ourselves and others, largely through the expression of our moral code; our Adult expresses our skills and knowledge, and processes information, often mediating between our own and others' conflicting Parent and Child; and our Child expresses our feelings, including our neurotic compulsions (which we often delude ourselves come from our "good" Parent). We move around among our ego states hour by hour and minute by minute throughout our waking lives.

People interact with each other through *transactions* between their ego states. Since each person may initiate a transaction from any of his or her three ego states and address any of the three ego states of another, there are nine possible ways in which we can initiate a transaction.

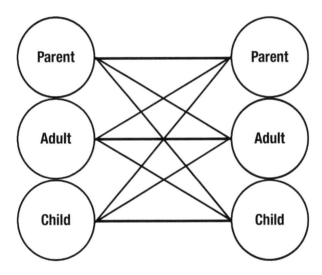

Two people, six ego states, nine possible transactions.

In practice, most transactions are Adult to Adult (emotion-free information exchange), Child to Child (emotionally charged exchange), Parent to Child (authoritative care and/or control), or Child to Parent (pleading with or complaining against authority). However, for the sake of inclusiveness, here is an archetypal example for each of the nine possible kinds of transaction.

"We must get a kid-proof lock on the bathroom cabinet." (Parent to Parent)

"Can you tell me the time?" (Adult to Adult)

"Let's make love." (Child to Child)

"Here, let me show you how to do that." (Parent to Adult)

"What's the best way to do this?" (Adult to Parent)

"Please may I have another biscuit?" (Child to Parent)

"No, you may not." (Parent to Child)

"I know you're very hungry. Supper will soon be ready." (Adult to Child)

"Oo, you are clever." (Child to Adult)

But the nature and meaning of even such simple transactions as the examples I have given are overwhelmingly determined by tone and body language as well as literal content. Try saying "Why?" in each of the nine possible ways.

Furthermore, many—perhaps most—transactions, and certainly the most interesting ones, are *duplex*, that is, *covert* and *overt* communications are occurring simultaneously. Such transactions are part of the healthy hypocrisy that informs much of civilised intercourse between people, protecting the participants from all kinds of discomfort; but in all such cases, the covert transaction is the true meaning of the communication. An archetypal example is, "Would you like to come in for a cup of coffee?" (Adult to Adult), which is really, "Let's have it off at my place" (Child to Child).

But covert transactions are also the stuff of the repetitive, maladaptive, pain-invoking communications we have with each other, and whose uncovering is a core task of psychotherapy. In the language of

Transactional Analysis, a *game* is a set series of covert (ulterior) transactions with predictable *negative payoffs* for each of the participants. Games are played by the *Adapted Child* ego states of the players, and although the overall process of different games may vary considerably, in all games the players move amongst only three roles, *Persecutor*, *Rescuer*, and *Victim*, switching roles in the course of the game but with each player always ending up in the role consistent with his or her most familiar negative payoff. While all of the roles are manifestations of the Adapted Child ego state, Persecutor masquerades as controlling Parent, Rescuer masquerades as nurturing Parent, and Victim masquerades as the authentic part of the Child ego state called the *Free Child*. We spot complementary players for our own games with amazing speed and precision across the most crowded room.

Through transactions with each other, we give and receive *strokes*, which nourish us and are as essential to our psychic survival as food is to our bodily survival. A *stroke* is any acknowledgement one person gives another, verbally or non-verbally. There are *unconditional positive strokes* ("I love you irrespective of anything you do to please or displease me"); *conditional positive strokes* ("If you tidy your room, I'll buy you a new pair of jeans"); *conditional negative strokes* ("Do that once more and you're grounded"); and *unconditional negative strokes* ("There's nothing you can do or say to please me"). Strokes are so essential to us that, as all parents and teachers know full well, we would rather receive negative strokes than no strokes at all.

All strokes reinforce the behaviour they are given for. Positive strokes reinforce behaviour and make the recipient feel good about him- or herself; negative strokes reinforce behaviour and make the recipient feel bad about him- or herself. Punishment (negative strokes) only momentarily suppresses the behaviour it is given for, while actually increasing the expression of that undesired behaviour in the future. Only by consistently ignoring, that is, giving no strokes at all, is undesired behaviour gradually extinguished. (Animal trainers have always known this anti-commonsense truth. Why don't we choose our political leaders from amongst animal trainers?)

We all have *positive* and *negative target strokes*, respectively the strokes that give us most pleasure and most pain, that most enlarge and most diminish our self-esteem. We acquired our positive target strokes through the overt and covert positive strokes we were given in early childhood; we acquired our negative target strokes through the overt and covert negative strokes we were given in early childhood. The positive strokes we received in early childhood, called our *permissions*, are associated with the authentic expression of our Free Child ego state; the negative strokes we received in early childhood, called our *injunctions*, are associated with the chronic and compulsive games we play with our Adapted Child, leading to our most painful payoffs.

The totality of the strokes we received to all our growing ego states in early childhood are called our *messages*, which we autonomously combined (with the use of our Adult) into the handful of existential decisions that constitute the core of our being.

On with the show!

CHAPTER ONE

Zeitgeist

In and out of time

It is unlikely that the total span of recorded history has been a long enough time for evolution to have wrought any noticeable changes in "human nature". Whenever and wherever people have recorded their reflections on the problems inherent in human beings' relationships with each other and the universe, the same difficulties and perplexities are met with the same solutions and wisdoms over and over again.

"There is nothing new under the sun" and much evidence of circularity in the "truths" espoused by human beings. Those people we call original thinkers usually utter old truths afresh in a voice better attuned to the tone of their own time. Copernicus revised the Greek idea of a Sun-centred universe; Darwinian evolutionary theory had been espoused by various others since before the Common Era; the unconscious mind had its place and was at home in literature long before Freud; and in matters pertaining to love, the advice expressed by Ovid two thousand years ago is as popular in today's magazines as it ever was. Apples falling on people's heads and causing uniquely revelational moments in human thought are a romantic myth.

Our contemporary voice

Notwithstanding the timelessness and immutability of our deepest concerns—love, death, meaning, fate, and free will—we are so constituted as to keep wondering and struggling to find better ways of understanding ourselves than have so far been achieved. In the parlance of today, this quest may be seen as a reflection of our homeostatic disposition, the constant pull–push of arousal and quiescence that is written into our biology and which has amongst its spin-offs all of art, science, and philosophy.

Probably the longest cycle in the history of ideas is the alternating orientations of holism and atomism. Although neither orientation has ever been entirely absent, the general tenor of human thought seems to have begun holistic and then started swinging towards atomistic about two and a half thousand years ago, apparently reaching its apogee in the twentieth century, from which time it has begun to turn. Physics seems to have reached the turning point first, expressed in Heisenberg's uncertainty principle and Einstein's theory of relativity, but biology is still engaged in the triumphalism of the human genome and atomistic brain research. And psychology, which only began to be atomistic when most other fields of endeavour were nearly finished with analysis, as an academic discipline is wildly out of step with the current Zeitgeist.

Outside academia, psychology seems to have found its contemporary voice by blending itself with philosophy and medicine, both of which fields have branches that seem precisely to reflect the compromises between materialism and mystery, determinism and choice that characterise humanity's present hovering outlook. In philosophy, existentialism is the name of the game; in medicine, it is homeopathy. Psychology that blends itself with these calls itself humanistic. Contemporarily, we are aware of the homeostatic balance between left-brain atomism and right-brain holism in what we call "New Age" thinking.

But the mundane reality of people's professional lives has lagged behind the movement of theories. The twentieth century was still one of increasing specialisation in which people were required to know more and more about less and less in order to procure their PhDs and ensure their viability in the employment market-place. In many subjects, knowledge continued to be particularised to its limits; and perhaps more importantly for the general human condition, academics and others became more and more unhappily isolated in the autism of their specialisms.

But towards the end of the twentieth century and continuing to the present, there has been a burgeoning of interdisciplinary conferences and cogent but popular writing about science that extends communication and nourishing strokes for intellectual givers and receivers alike. It is no longer infra dig for academics to step out of their ivory towers and communicate simply with the intelligent lay public. Not only has this represented a backlash against the loneliness of those whose expertise is ultra-specialised; it is also a manifestation of a contemporary cultural climate in which academia is called upon to justify the funds it receives, and academic salaries are relatively low. Books such as James Gleich's *Chaos* (1988), John Gray's *Straw Dogs* (2002), and Dava Sobel's *Longitude* (2007), as well as many science-made-easy television programmes, have flourished, and such authors and television present-ers are now envied rather than disdained by their col-leagues for their popular acclaim and monetary gain.

While the particular preoccupations of any age may be seen with hindsight to be transient or even trivial, to the people alive at a given time they are impera-tively demanding of attention. Though I am conscious of the unavoidable blinkeredness of my own here-and-now perspective, I believe there are a number of con-temporary conditions that are stretching our innate adaptability to critical limits. Those of us alive today are suffering the Chinese curse, "May you live in inter-esting times".

Population explosion

By far the biggest change in human consciousness over the past fifty years has been the emergence of uni-versal awareness of the world's population explosion. This was not the case even in the 1950s. Especially in Australia, where I was then living, there was plenty of room for everybody, full employment, and government hoardings that exhorted us to "populate or perish". Our individual existences were valued and useful to the col-lective, we knew we were needed and so were full of buoyant self-esteem.

Now, we all know there are far too many of us and the world could well do without us individually. Collec-tively, self-esteem is low, especially among the working classes whose unskilled labour has greatly diminished in value. In the developed countries with which we are familiar, the contented, conservative, reliable, con-scientious working-class personality, full of pride and dignity, has been replaced by a personality type that is envious, bitter, pugnacious, amoral, hostile, and despairing. As a species, we have become like rats in an overcrowded cage.

The most extreme outcome of this critically unstable scenario is that, one way or another, like countless other species, we will fail to rise to the challenge and will become extinct. Yet there is already a spontaneous corrective response to our crisis of overpopulation that suggests we may save ourselves. Notwithstanding the desperate bids of many infertile couples to overcome their infertility with the aid of science, there are now many people—and especially women—who are voluntarily renouncing parenthood out of their own free will. This was virtually unheard of when I was first married fifty years ago, when having babies was the unreflective desire of all couples; and the small proportion of infertile couples would almost surely adopt the surplus of unwanted births as quickly as possible. Although the rise in declared homosexuality in some developed countries is clearly associated with its decriminalisation, it may be that its rise is factual as well as apparent, that is, an unconscious collective response to the world's population crisis. And the proscription in China against having more than one child certainly suggests that a species-preservative adaptation is under way.

Even the use of "weapons of mass destruction" may have an ecological purpose. Only time will tell; but we are meanwhile faced with the here-and-now reality of many individuals with deeply undermined self-esteem associated with their perception of their personal redundancy. Responsively, it behoves us, as therapists and counsellors, empathically to philosophise with our clients on this contemporary contingency of the human condition.

The death of God

For the whole of recorded history, mankind has found in its gods and their commandments the justification of turning away timidly rather than braving the excitement and terror of uncertainty. The major monotheistic religions counteract all our fears of uncertainty in espousing an all-loving, omniscient, omnipotent, omnipresent God to whom we are obliged. Conceptually, we are thus made safe and certain; pragmatically, the commandments of God leave us little scope, if we are obedient, for doing much that might excitingly imperil our lives. If those who flout God's commandments seem to survive His wrath unscathed, in societies where judicial legislature is religious, punishment is meted out by human judges in the name of God; in societies where secular authorities are less vengeful towards sinners, the obedient majority are reassured that the sinner will at least receive his or her just deserts in the world to come. Psychologically speaking, the function of religion is to console us by justifying the sacrifices of adventure and excitement that we make for the sake of safety.

Our fear of death—and of the unknown generally—which is, throughout the world, rationalised and justified by our obedience to our understanding of God's will, is intellectual as well as physical. Not only must we do and not do certain things in order to avoid punishment in this world or the next; we are also required to have pure thoughts and to refrain from heresy. God's own punishment for a too open mind is insanity. For public heresies, men are publically punished—at least made to recant; for heresies that take place in the privacy of a man's mind, the influence of God within him persuades him to make public his confession, or at least to experience the private punishment of guilt.

In the last hundred years or so, the Western world has become, at least nominally, a great deal more secular. For individual human beings, it now seems possible—perhaps for the first time in history—to disavow the existence of God without being out of line with the ethos of the culture. Humanism espouses "enlightened self-interest" as the new rationalisation of the old, God-imposed controls on our self- and other-destructive impulses, but increasing competition for jobs and homes, and the tenuousness of sexual relationships, seem to have invoked in us self-interest that tends to be more unbridled than "enlightened".

Our new-found collective willingness to challenge the authority of God is less courageous than it superficially appears. At least until very recently, we were able to relinquish the reassurance of God only by replacing it with the reassurance of science. During the course of the few centuries since the Renaissance, God has trembled at the presumed insults to Him by men of science, most notably by Copernicus, Darwin, and Freud, who respectively disavowed man's centrality in the universe, his specialness as a species, and his self-awareness. At first, God fought back valiantly, bringing down His wrath on hubristic mankind in the form of the Black Death and sundry other collective calamities, and on particular men and women in the form of inquisitions, burnings, and derision. But by the beginning of the twentieth century, the theories of science could confidently account for the most horrendous acts of God in materialistic terms. To very many more people than ever before, God was toppled and presumed dead.

But the new-found materialistic security of human consciousness has been very quickly found wanting. In the wake of Heisenberg's uncertainty principle, Einstein's theory of relativity and post-Einsteinian cosmologies, full of uncertainties and such nihilistic horrors as black holes, have permeated the everyday existential conscious-nesses of large numbers of people. Without God to fall back on, we are left trembling at Nothing.

We are presently left floundering around in our quest for certainty and meaning in a choppy sea of possi-bilities. As yet, our lack of resolution is expressed in a primitively volatile mixture of despairing nihilism and despotic religious fundamentalism.

Fundamentalism is the bid to make God a fact, like scientific knowledge. Its literalism misses the point that there cannot be just one interpretation of any-thing. Out of its adherents' desperate terror of death, fundamentalism avows the absolute one and only truth with absolute certainty of eternal life through privi-leged absolute knowledge of God. Unavoidably, it must righteously murder all infidels, whose mere existence threatens its precariously teetering security.

But notwithstanding the perils of fundamentalism, there is also peril in nihilism. Absoluteness, which is the ugly defence against existential terror, unites the two extremes. Dogmatic atheism and religious fun-damentalism are opposites that are identical in their expression of contemporary spiritual disease.

The dissolution of trust

In parallel to the dissolution of our trust in God—the super-duper Parent who makes everything all right in the end—we are also beset by the dissolution of trust in and respect for secular authority.

Professionalism is a function of the Parent ego state, encompassing the balance of caring responsibility and autonomous authority. A hundred years ago there were few professions, and the professions there were—doctors, lawyers, teachers, and the clergy—were revered and trusted for their unquestionable integrity and selfless concern for the people they served. Now, professionalism is democratised to include multitudes whose orientation is me-first Child rather than you-first Parent, so we feel justified in *mis*trusting the plethora of "servants" we rely upon to keep our cars, televisions, computers, plumbing, and roofs in states of repair; and we also call to account the traditional professions there were, discounting their authority and suspecting their integrity. Constant invigilation insults professional autonomy; complaints procedures abound; professionals who touch those in their care risk being charged with criminal abuse; targets are set for doctors and teachers as if they were manufacturers of consumer goods. The frightened Child in us all escalates its rebellious tyranny in the name of freedom while actually desperately seeking the containment of a confidently and lovingly controlling Parent. And the deposed Parent, divested of authority and respect, resorts to indemnity policies against litigation, or else bows out completely. At the time of writing (November 2010), according to a recent survey, one-third of teachers say they want to leave their profession within the next five years, and one-quarter of doctors want to quit their jobs. In America, in some high-risk areas of medical practice like neurosurgery, doctors are choosing to retire early rather than pay malpractice insurance premiums of up to $200,000 per annum.

For psychotherapists, too, litigious action has become a constant risk and, even when not threatened legally, therapists are regularly taken to task and even disenfranchised by ethical committees which no longer tend to support their practitioners against complainants but, in the interest of protecting their politically correct status, fearfully presume the Child/Victim to be "right". The deeply mutually challenging, complexly private relationship between therapist and patient, whereby the therapist plays out the controlling and nurturing Parent to the needy Child of the patient and to the satisfaction of both of them, has been democratised to "helper and client" and fast approaches "seller and customer", which, in the context of psychotherapy, means the "customer" does not get what he or she most needs.

Undoubtedly, there are abuses of Parental power—in the home and in society at large—that need to be addressed and dealt with by any civilised society; and maybe our present *Zeitgeist* in this regard is a backlash against such abuses in previous generations. Nevertheless, I maintain that our present *Zeitgeist* is an extreme that both reflects and reinforces the profound existential dis-ease that is the hallmark of our time. A psychotherapist today is challenged to go against the politically correct orthodoxies and to be the stalwart, confident, assertive, authoritative Parent that his or her patients/clients are deeply seeking.

Parents and children

As for God and professional practitioners of all kinds, ordinary parents are today undermined in their authority and unconfident in their role.

Materialism

It used to be the case that children stayed innocent of greedy materialism at least until their teenage years, when their desire for fashionable clothes and other possessions bears witness to their burgeoning need for sexual display. But in response to the market forces of capitalism, communicated to children principally through television advertising, over the past forty or fifty years children have become "consumers" and "customers" at ever-earlier ages, their innocence ruthlessly exploited by canny manufacturers of "must-haves" for every tiny tot. Birthday parties can no longer be simple celebrations, but every one competitively elaborate and expensive.

In the face of these forces, the most puritanical of parents find it virtually impossible to deprive their children of the goods that "everybody" has; and those parents who, by dint of poverty, are unable to provide these goods know the cruel scorn and humiliation their children will experience in the playground.

And rarely is it possible today for the income of one parent to suffice for a family's needs. Most mothers are obliged to have at least part-time paid employment to meet the enormous cost of paying the mortgage, which is the average family's anxious obsession.

Harassed togetherness

Until about thirty years ago, when they were not at school, children "went out to play", freely adventuring with other children who lived nearby. Typically, children left the house soon after breakfast, sometimes returning briefly for lunch but often taking picnic supplies with them, and only returning home in the late afternoon. They lived in the wonderland of imaginative play and the invigorating largesse of physical exploration of the outdoor environment. And the vast majority of children walked or cycled to school on their own, wrapped in the privacy of their autonomous selfhood.

Now, in the name of both safety and practicality, children are rarely separated from their parents, and both parents and children—whose activities and conversations are naturally so often boring to each other —are bound, often for hours every day, to be locked together in the confines of a car, in mutual irritation and frustrated freedom, as the children are fetched and carried to school, to distant friends, and to attendance at the numerous activities by which their days are programmed. For parents and children, respite from each others' company tends to be limited to the hours children plonk themselves in front of computers or television, locked in couch-potato virtual reality. Despite all our domestic machinery designed for human ease and comfort, daily life is enormously more confined and anxious than it used to be.

Moral relativity

In parallel to the dissolution of trust between grown-ups, few children today express automatic deference or respect towards adults by virtue of the disparity of their ages. We now live in a Child-led rather than a Parent-led culture.

Until about forty years ago, children, generally without prompting, surrendered their seats on buses or elsewhere to adults; now, many don't even do so for the obviously old or frail. Teachers could count on the explicit endorsement of their authority by the parents of their pupils; now they are often abused and attacked by some parents as well as children. Moral relativity is politically *de rigueur*. Adults are no longer consensually united in their moral values and codes of behaviour, leaving children—and the Child in all of us—anxiously bereft of the security of authoritative containment.

Sex

Today, we are free to be monogamous or polygamous, heterosexual, bisexual, or homosexual, single or joint parents, and all these options are displayed and purveyed through the devices of capitalism as available commodities. Notwithstanding that most adults, through their deeper instinctual and experiential wisdom, abjure the despair and nihilism associated with untrammelled sexual licence, children are constantly bombarded with "the facts", which they can cope with only through precocious and specious awareness.

First five-year-old: Guess what I found on our patio this morning? A used condom.
Second five-year-old: What's a patio?

As witnesses to their parents' serial sexual relationships, multitudes of children are burdened with the primal anxiety associated with explicitly knowing the manifest reality of their parents' sexual behaviour. And there are few parents left who have the conviction or the courage to exhort their teenage children to pre-marital chastity in the name of idealism. Aids has become the only warning deterrent against free-and-easy sexual behaviour.

Materialism, harassed togetherness, moral relativism, and precocious sexual awareness together make contemporary parenthood an uncertainly demanding task; and many seek—implicitly, if not explicitly—the guidance of confidently non-conformist counsellors, willing to offer them the permission to express confident control as well as *laissez-faire* in response to the impulses of their children.

The burden of choice

Secular existentialism burdens us with choice. Today, not only are we free shamelessly to be and to do as we please in sexual matters, but in virtually every other aspect of our lives as well.

Notwithstanding that by the beginning of the twentieth century the constraints of religious observance were rapidly declining in favour of passionate devotion to the freedoms made available by science and technology, habit died hard, and most people still, however perfunctorily, regularly and dutifully attended places of worship. So, too, was secular daily life contained in the obsessively ritualistic timetabling of washing, ironing, cleaning, baking, visiting relatives, going for drives in the country … and most people ate fish on Fridays, roast beef and Yorkshire pudding on Sundays, and a very limited range of meals on the other days of the week as well. Until the 1960s, life was ritualised to an extent almost unbelievable to those too young to remember. The absence of choice bound everything in place through ceremony and continuity.

When Paris dictated the length of our hemlines, when we were not allowed to leave the table until everybody had finished, when children called all familiar but unrelated adults "auntie" or "uncle", when strawberries in August were a treat, when couples—at least nominally—refrained from full sexual congress until they were married, and we were generally obliged to conform to the consensually agreed values and constraints of society as a whole, we hid our deviances in willing hypocrisy (hypocrisy being the homage that vice pays to virtue). Thus we were free to concentrate on things that really mattered to us as individuals, unencumbered by the numbing demand of forever having to choose.

Contemporary individualistic freedom, reinforced by material abundance, cruelly demands of the two-year-old in each of us, "Vanilla, chocolate, or strawberry?" We even have to choose amongst a plethora of forms of therapy for our diseases, with "non-directive, person-centred" counselling ironically espoused as the most politically correct form of therapy even for those whose suffering is a direct consequence of their very incapacity to choose.

Speed

We are homeostatic organisms, inescapably swinging between arousal and quiescence for as long as we are alive. We apply thousands of words to this basic dichotomy, with which we elaborate it into a large range of discrete experiences, which are evaluated largely by reference to context. Being aroused when we haven't eaten for five hours becomes "hungry"; in response to a threatening stimulus, we are "frightened"; in anticipation of fulfilled desire, we are "excited"; in response to the blocking of desire, we are "frustrated"; in response to the unexpected blocking of desire, we are "disappointed".

Our pleasures are contained in the transitional moment of quiescence consequent on the fulfilment of desire, before the memory of desire is quite faded and before the movement that is called being alive propels us to chase after another desire. Desire seeks its fulfilment in pleasure, but pleasure is not guaranteed. Intrinsic to the process is the risk of failure and an associated degree of pain proportional to the pleasure sought. Maximum pleasure for extraverts is associated with relatively large amounts of arousing stimulation; maximum pleasure for introverts is associated with relatively large amounts of quiescence.

Until lately in human history, one of the chief balancers of speed, excitement, and adventure in our lives was the predictability, order, and safety of religion, its proscriptions and its prescribed rituals. Pilgrimages and holy wars provided participants with a satisfying blend of dangerous excitement and safe discipline through the life-risking dangers of travel and war and the immutable conviction of righteous certainty in the name of God's will and protection. The latter-day equivalent is travelling in the name of Work, with lower levels of both commitment and excitement than en route to a Crusade, but with a fair homeostatic balance maintained.

With or without benefit of an obsessively informed mission, travelling is a universally and timelessly popular means of satisfying our episodic needs for stepping outside the safe, established structure of our lives into speedy excitement. But implicit in the promises of travel is that the planning and effort we invest in the process is proportional to the pleasurable excitement of adventure and novelty that we achieve.

Before the invention of the steam engine and the bicycle, the greatest attainable speed for human beings was that of a horse, and the best possible comfort and safety in a closed vehicle pulled by a horse over roads incomparably bumpier than our present-day worst. But a few miles' travel could reward us with a novelty value—changed culture, changed dialect—that we now have to travel long distances to achieve.

As well as the increased speed (and decreased novelty) with which we are now able to move our bodies, we also have telephones, faxes, mobile phones, e-mail, the internet … designed primarily to give us forms of communication previously undreamt of. They also, incidentally, add ever-increasing speed to every facility with which they provide us. So speed has become an addiction in our lives, a substance—like cigarettes or drugs—whose ingestion we are persuaded is the means of satisfying our appetite for time, but which provides only fleeting illusions of time gained while creating an ever-increasing craving for it.

While much of our contemporary addiction to actual speed can be attributed to the speed that is intrinsically valued in the products of technology, some of it is also a compensation for the diminishment of excitement (which is biologically equivalent to speed) inherent in the novelties of the changing seasons.

Central heating and air-conditioning make our lives optimally physically comfortable throughout the year; we are continuously offered a super-abundance of foods from around the world; and our gluttonous appetite for television cookery programmes testifies to our need for ever more sophisticated novelty in our daily food to compensate for the no longer existent pleasures of seasonally limited delicacies like strawberries and asparagus, and the novelties of previously untried foods when we travelled abroad. Now, at home and abroad, high streets are swamped by multi-national chains purveying identical goods. And even the most challenging physical adventures like climbing Mount Everest have been made almost safe, easy, and commonplace.

Fast food, fast cars, fast sex, fast money, fast divorce, and fast celebrity are the order of the day. The Far East and the Antipodes have become *de rigueur* minimum requirements for European youth in search of their adventures; and we are fast running out of novel possibilities on Earth—witness the space tourist who paid £14,000,000 for the exclusively better, more distant, and more exciting adventure of accompanying two astronauts on their scientific mission.

So speed and busyness dominate our lives, our diaries being fuller into the more and more distant future. Addictively, we grasp for time in our specious bid to overcome the anxiety that our technological time-savers have created. The integrity of our nervous systems is at stake.

Ironically, obsessive religious fundamentalism is one form of homeostatic backlash against the excesses of danger and speed. But suicide bombing represents the implosion of speed and compulsiveness at the limit of both—which is death. More gently, there is continuing growth in the popularity of quiescent activities such as transcendental meditation, the self-discipline of perfecting our bodies at the gym, and obsessiveness about maintaining our health and fitness and prolonging our lives through diet and dietary supplements. Self-regulation of our homeostatic need to balance exciting speed and calm self-discipline is beginning to gain ground again at life-enhancing levels of opposition and tension between them.

We live in interesting times!

CHAPTER TWO

Believing

This chapter is about the Parent ego state. As its name suggests, the Parent ego state in all of us in relation to our own and others' Child ego states is nearly, if not absolutely, congruent with the responsibilities and privileges of mothers and fathers in their relationships to their children. For the therapist in doubt about his or her rights and obligations to clients, reference to the archetype of parents and their children is a reliable guide.

Professionalism

A hundred years ago, in the absence of antibiotics and central heating, life was shorter and physically much more uncomfortable than today. Nevertheless, self-sufficiency was for most people possible most of the time, whereas today the sophisticated demands we have for our health, comfort, and amusement feel like survival needs, and we are ever more dependent on others to provide and maintain what have become essentials in our lives.

Thus was born professionalism, which is nurturing, reassuring know-how. We are nearly all professionals now, each purveying some small Parent ego state expertise in response to our ever-expanding imperative Child needs that only others can supply. Implicit in nearly every payment we now make to another is the agitated cry, "I'm helpless, make it better for me", from the computer repair man to our personal trainers, gym instructors, plastic surgeons, and financial advisors. Survival is ever more psychological and feels ever more frighteningly tenuous.

Being a professional of any kind means *confidently and reassuringly looking after people in some way that they need to be looked after, in return for money paid*. In seeking out the plumber to unblock our sink, the accountant to sort out our tax return, the dentist to fix our teeth, the taxi driver to get us to the airport in a hurry, the hairdresser to make us beautiful … what we are looking for, above all else, is that person's *assurance* that what we hope for can be done and that he or she is capable of and willing to do it for us *promptly*. If we have the choice between any two professionals equally competent in their skills, we always choose—and choose again—the one who makes us feel secure in his or her *confident care* of us in the fulfilment of our needs.

And nowhere is the need for the caring aspect of professionalism more pronounced than in those areas of our lives that concern our physical or psychological health and wellbeing. People consult doctors, dentists, and therapists of all kinds with some, however unfounded, anxiety or even apprehension, and it behoves us, as professionals, immediately on meeting them (and even before, if a telephone appointment is made), to reduce and, if possible, eliminate their anxiety by the reassurance of our *smiles, tone of voice, and the words we choose*.

The profession of psychotherapy

A hundred years ago to today

The profession of psychotherapy began with Freud's psychoanalysis about a hundred years ago. The *Zeitgeist* of that time was as extremely Parent-oriented—authoritative, inhibiting, deferential—as we are today extremely Child-oriented—democratic, defiant of constraint, self-expressive. In his practice, Freud saw much of his task to be the liberation of his patients from their diseases associated with the excessive suppression and repression of their most atavistic sexual and aggressive impulses, although (contrary to much popular misunderstanding) he never advocated the acting out of these impulses; and he lived his own life in a rigorously puritanical manner.

With his first analysands, Freud had open, friendly, and even sociable relationships, and most analyses were completed in a few weeks or months. It was only as *transference* revealed itself that it became apparent that it was a central feature of the process of curing nervous ailments. Out of this discovery, the blank poker-faced projective screen of the analyst was invented as a *de rigueur* requirement of being an analyst, which has continued to the present day.

From then on, in the hands of subsequent generations of practitioners—as in all originally inspirational, creative movements—psychoanalysis became, as theory and therapy, increasingly bureaucratised and lengthy. Eventually, about forty years ago, it began to lose its credibility. Its practitioners became stultified in their rigidity of procedure, and those who submitted to it were largely limited to the self-indulgently narcissistic and the rich who could afford the time and money to spend years in self-absorption.

But people continued to have psychological problems and the need of experts to help them solve them. Few in today's secular world are sufficiently religiously observant to resort to seeking and accepting the traditional equivalent counsel of priests, rabbis, or mullahs, so the profession of psychotherapy has stayed alive, albeit in forms that have of necessity adapted to the spirit of our age.

Irrespective of theory, people need and demand their problems to be heard and dealt with quickly and relatively cheaply. Even in America where, until recently, health insurers accepted the necessarily long-term nature of psychotherapy, and paid up accordingly, this is no longer the case. A few weeks or months is all that is allowed, and therapists are required regularly and frequently to justify the continuance of treatment for every patient. Expediency rules. Short-term therapeutic goals and procedures are the order of the day, and the profession has rationalised and justified its adaptation in terms of "ego psychology", which finds merit in dealing with the face-value level of people's problems rather than assuming that "real cure" can only be achieved by the lengthy process of accessing pre-verbal infantile memories.

Nevertheless, psychoanalysis as *theory* informs virtually all forms of contemporary psychotherapy, and my own experience is that Freud's theoretical genius, and the theory of the Oedipus conflict in particular, are validated in every encounter I have in the privacy of my own practice.

Rules and regulations

A large proportion of the responsibilities and privileges of the psychotherapist is the setting of clear-cut, firm limitations as a preliminary to embarking on their therapeutic relationships.

Notwithstanding the current "customer is always right" ethos in society at large, the deep, timeless truth is that responsibility and authority are promised to each other. You *are* more competent at living than your clients—at least in the areas in which they consult you—or else what is your use to them and why are they paying you?

The absurd extreme of "child rights" was demonstrated a few years ago in the report of a fifteen-year-old Scottish girl who filed a lawsuit claiming that detentions she received at school contravened Article 5 of the European Convention on Human Rights, specifically that clause which protects children from degrading treatment!

Nevertheless, as an autonomous adult who will be paying you for your services, the client has an obvious right to accept or reject what you have to offer. To this extent, it behoves you to declare, in a preliminary session, what rules will apply if the relationship is agreed, and to openly answer any questions the potential client puts to you that will enable her to decide whether or not to embark on the relationship.

In accordance with your own precepts and values, you will be more or less willing to negotiate some terms; but it is ultimately your responsibility and privilege to decide the rules to which the client must submit if the relationship is to begin.

In the democratised world of political correctness, the power you will thus be presuming is speciously taken to be an insulting humiliation of the client and a negation of the "equality" between you. The politically incorrect reality is that, although we are all ultimately equal in our humanity, the specific role relationships of our lives are not all equal to equal, but just as often of a kind whereby there are those who give orders and those who obey, which is a symbiotic arrangement for the benefit of both parties.

This truth was vividly portrayed in the famous Stanford Prison Experiment conducted at Stanford University in 1971. Volunteers were divided into "prisoners" and "warders" for an agreed period of two weeks. The only agreed taboo was on any form of physical violence. As part of the experiment, after a few days during which warders and prisoners played out their conventional roles, the warders were instructed to begin a new "democratic" relationship to the prisoners. The inability of both warders and prisoners to cope with this new regime, and the ensuing mayhem, forced the premature conclusion of the experiment.

The truth that in the mundane role relationships of life "some people are more equal than others" does *not* imply negative discrimination, exploitation, scapegoating, or eugenics.

Setting goals

If not at a preliminary meeting with a client, then certainly very soon after, it is useful for both you and her to define the goal or goals of your relationship. This can be recorded in your notes and referred to whenever doubt or confusion arises as to just what the process that is going on between you is all about. I find it best to treat the goals set as tentative, that is, valid until the client and therapist agree that the goals have been achieved (and new goals are set or therapy is terminated), or the client chooses to redefine her goals. Therapists need to insist that goals set are tangible, that is, when achieved will be observably so to the therapist (and other intimates in the client's life) as well as in the subjective awareness of the client. Acceptable contracts, for example, might be "To get and stay out of debt", "To feel comfortable in and enjoy social situations", "To finish my degree", "To be in harmony with my husband/wife in bringing up our children", but not abstract and vague like "To improve my self-knowledge" or "To be happy". The stuff of psychotherapy is itself an abstract and intangible "commodity", so creating tangible goals within it helps confirm that something "real" is being paid for in time and money.

Money and love

Within the context of the intimacy that develops between therapist and client, the therapist is always vulnerable to the charge that the "love" he or she offers is monetarily motivated. In all other healthy intimate relationships, love is given reciprocally rather than exchanged for money.

As the client discloses his deepest self and vulnerabilities to the therapist, and so becomes attached to her in a very intimate way, it is understandable that a part of him will resent that the "worth" he has to the therapist is principally pecuniary. His self-esteem is diminished by this awareness, much as it might be for a man who pays a prostitute for sex. There is truth in this perception, which the honest therapist admits, but it is to be hoped that the therapist (as a true professional) values her work for the intrinsic satisfactions it brings her as well as for the money she earns by it. To deny to the client that she values the money given is a transparent falsehood that will undermine the client's respect for her. Rather, when appropriate, she should acknowledge this fact but equally avow that there is much else she also gets from the client, including the healing of her own wounds. She might also point out that there are clients she would choose not to take on, irrespective of payment offered to her. For the authenticity of this claim to be appreciated by the client, it helps if the therapist has a waiting list!

Some clients—usually those who are doing battle with their perceptions of themselves as having very little worth to others—will so resent paying the therapist that they will, in various devious ways, seek to avoid payment or, in extreme cases, demand refunds for therapy already paid for on the grounds that the therapist has done them no good at all, or even that she has done them harm. Such ploys should always be responded to with the utmost confidently controlling Parent. As professionals, we are *paid for our time*, and, as for all other professionals, our clients are obliged to pay for our time irrespective of their assessment of the value or lack of value they have received for their money.

I remember one client I had—a man who projected a great deal of resentful anger onto the world in general and me in particular—who pre-emptively left therapy owing me £90 and, despite my numerous telephone calls to him, refused to pay me. I knew from my acquired knowledge of him that in his relationship to me he had achieved the psychological payoff typical of all his relationships, namely righteous triumph (which was, of course, a pyrrhic victory bought at the cost of alienation and the enmity of others). I was enraged and decided to get my revenge by getting my £90, and achieving power over his aggression that I had failed to achieve when he was in therapy, and thus denying him his triumph. I went through the formal procedure of the small claims court, a prescribed step-by-step process, at every stage of which my client could have voluntarily paid his debt. He ignored all the chances the process gave him. Eventually, when the bailiff walked into the men's clothing shop my client owned and began taking jackets and jumpers in lieu of his debt, he wrote a cheque—for his debt and costs. *I* was triumphant and maybe, I told myself, it was the most effective piece of therapy I had done with him.

For readers who are sufficiently tough-minded, I recommend avoiding bad debts by agreeing with clients that they pay in advance for their sessions. But some combination of my Parent and Adapted Child messages have always made me more comfortable only requiring payment for my services after they have been delivered.

Therapists and friends

Therapists are more than friends and less than friends. They are more than friends in knowing their clients more deeply than friends do. They are less than friends in the limits they set on their availability to their clients and the payment they accept for the care, support, and goodwill they give.

We choose lovers for the tension of oppositeness between us; we choose friends for the similarities between us. Although in all our relationships *parts* of one person connect significantly with *parts* of another (and other parts connect with parts of other people), by and large we can rely on our friends to be similar to us in important ways and to stand up for us when the going gets rough. So, too, can we rely on our therapists—except when we can't!

Although our friends may be aware of our hang-ups and chide us for the repetitive ways we express them, beyond a certain point, when we begin to feel more criticised than understood, they stop. Our friendship is too valuable to them to threaten it with "the truth, the whole truth, and nothing but the truth". This is the point where the therapist takes over. It is a crucial part of the therapist's job to stretch the boundaries of his client's being with confrontations that the client will inevitably defend against with multitudinous "Yes buts" and quite likely with hostile feelings towards the therapist and a strong desire to terminate the relationship.

But, of course, this is the hump where true therapy begins and the therapist, like any loving parent towards his children, has to accept being *disliked*, often intensely. And this is when, in truth, the client begins to get his money's worth. The difference here between parents and children and therapists and clients is that—by and large—children don't run away, but clients can and often do. Successfully working through deep confrontation of the client's responsibility for his pains is the greatest creative challenge of being a psychotherapist.

Physician heal thyself

Paradoxically, being disliked is often hardest for the kind of people who choose to become psychotherapists. While the styles of different therapists may vary hugely, there is a deep level at which they are often united. Many psychotherapists—including the best—have chosen the profession out of their need to heal their own deepest wound of feeling unloveworthy. Many therapists, one way or another, felt required, as children, to be more grown-up and giving than is appropriate to childhood. Often, they had a sick or otherwise needy parent whom they sought to "make better", playing down their own needs for nourishing, unconditional love. And becoming a psychotherapist is a continuation of that role, a profound need to *earn love* through making others "better" and "happy".

In a therapist's confrontation of a client that, however temporarily, makes the client unhappier rather than happier, the therapist is often challenging her own deepest Adapted Child neurotic compulsion, that is, being a Rescuer to the client's Victim. The game Rescuers play is that of trying to do for another what the other is capable of and needs to do for himself. The Rescuer's behaviour interferes with the other's self-actualisation, and the other resents and rejects the Rescuer's interference. The Rescuer ends up the hurt Victim of the other's Persecutor. Every time a therapist is tempted to—but resists—Rescuing a client, she is probably confronting and transmuting her own deepest neurotic compulsion and becoming more of an authentic helper.

Individuals, couples, families, and groups

Most potential clients declare that they want individual, not group, therapy. This desire is rationalised in various ways, including, of course, their desire for undivided attention as well as their inhibitions about disclosing themselves amongst strangers whom they may dislike or who might otherwise discomfort them. Yet individuality itself is formed in the social context of the family, as also are our hang-ups, and the therapy group can provide a quasi-ideal family in which all the shortcomings of our original family are negated. For everybody except those whose depression or anxiety is so great as to prevent them functioning acceptably at a social level,

I maintain that group therapy is to be preferred over individual therapy. Therapists may at first have to persuade clients of this fact, although it helps to point out how much cheaper group therapy will be for the client—not to mention that it earns the therapist more!

Group therapy opens up people's awareness of the differences and samenesses between themselves and others. The group is a microcosm of the world in which the client can express her personality assets and liabilities in the presence of insightful but accepting and essentially non-critical witnesses. Human beings are group animals. Moreover, although the therapist is always attributed the greatest (magical) power, for each client in a group of, say, six to eight (a number that is sufficient to achieve and maintain a sense of group cohesiveness but is smaller than a crowd) there are all these people in addition to the therapist ready and willing to help.

Furthermore, at the confrontational level of therapy, the consensual agreement of members of the group helps the therapist in his task by facing the client with the unassailably agreed truth of the issues he needs to face. And when there is consensual disagreement with the therapist—a permission all good group therapists encourage in a spirit of mutual openness and trust—the therapist enhances the respect his clients feel for him in his human willingness to be mistaken.

For each client, "giving" and "taking" find their balance in the setting of the group. Very often, people begin group therapy confused about the concepts of "giving" and "taking", evidenced in apologies they are prone to make for "taking too much of the group's time" in airing and seeking help for their own problems. Implicitly, they tend to divide the length of the session by the number of people in the group and feel entitled to "take" only their share. But they quickly learn that much of their "taking" is in fact "giving" of themselves to others, and that in free and spontaneous transactions with others the polarities disappear in a blend that is equally gratifying to all the participants.

Only children particularly benefit from group therapy, although, of course, they are most resistant to it. Out of their deprivation of the give and take of sibling love, hate, rivalry, aggression, and negotiation, no matter how socially well adjusted they may superficially be, all only children are deeply inept in Child to Child trans-actions. In the group setting, they, more than others, either self-centredly demand all the attention of the therapist or else over-reticently withdraw into silence. The group experience is a particular challenge to them and can rectify their deficient childhood experience.

One particularly interesting way of forming a group is with couples who feel the need to work through issues in their relationships with each other as well as to actualise themselves as individuals. A four-couple group can be a wonderfully stimulating and produc-tive experience for all the participants. Although, in principle, there is no need to preclude a couple within a group of individuals, in practice that couple's interac-tions with each other do tend, unfairly, to dominate the proceedings.

There are, of course, individuals who are too dis-turbed to participate in group therapy, which might be thought of as therapy for the three-to-six-year-old in each of the clients. Clients who are extremely depressed or anxious are in need of therapy for the pre-three-year-old in themselves, and individual therapy fulfils that need, granting them the undivided maternal-type nourishment, without which they will remain unable to rise to the challenge of the eroticised social world. A good therapeutic plan for such clients is to nourish them through their acute anxiety or depression in indi-vidual therapy and then promote them into a group.

Whether clients are in individual or group therapy, as they begin to change in profound ways, the balance of their intimate relationships outside therapy will invariably be disturbed. Many a resentful intimate other has declared, "You were all right until you started that bloody therapy." To this extent, I believe it behoves the therapist, if possible, to speak early on in the therapy to the intimate partners of their clients and warn them of the almost inevitable disruption to the equilibrium of their relationship through the process of therapy. While, ideally, the partner is contemporaneously in therapy, if not, it seems to me to be a matter of fairness to keep such partners informed and to welcome their questions concerning the changes taking place in the client. Permission for this needs, of course, to be obtained from the client, but I have rarely come across clients who deny me that permission, and most welcome the interest of their partners in the changes they are making in themselves.

Like group therapy, family therapy can be exceptionally interesting and rewarding in its complex dynamics. When therapists are consulted concerning the difficult or disturbed behaviour of a child, this is often largely attributable to a lack of Parent to Parent agreement in matters of principle and practice between the parents. In such cases, facilitating the parents in understanding and compromising over their differences, and thus presenting an unassailable united front to their child, can often rapidly solve the problems of the child.

Essential agreements

Before embarking on any therapeutic relationship, it is of the utmost importance to make clear to the potential client your rules and regulations that will apply throughout the course of therapy. This is the time for the client to raise her objections to any of your rules and to negotiate terms with you (to the extent that you are willing) and to ask any questions whose answers may be pertinent to her accepting or declining your offer of therapy. Following are outlines of issues usually declared by most therapists.

No sex or violence

Though these taboos may seem unnecessary to declare to most clients, they are worth stating. This is the *id* stuff that represents the biggest risk to your own and your clients' safety, especially in the context of the group. The eruption of violence may be threatened when clients are profoundly challenged. And sexual relationships formed in the group are likely to have very unhealthy underpinnings. Having contained these risks by explicit agreement, there may be occasions when you will be glad to have done so.

Confidentiality

I personally assume confidentiality and am always a little suspicious of the paranoid tendency of some potential clients who ask about it. My first response to such an enquiry is to ask why they are so concerned. Sometimes it is due to a client's legitimate worry that he may be compromised in his career advancement should his employers be aware that he is in need of psychotherapy, although this is rare in today's world. Generally, I give my assurance of confidentiality with the proviso that, at my own discretion, I would breach this agreement if I felt the client's wellbeing depended on it (such as if he were threatening suicide) or if he had committed a criminal act. Furthermore, I admit that, without disclosing the client's identity, I might usefully say to another client, "I have a client who ..." in the interest of pointing out to the other client my experience of a particular problem and ways of dealing with it.

Reciprocally, I expect of the client that he will respect the private depth of my relationship with him by agreeing not to seek judgement of my professional competence or ethical behaviour pre-emptively with any other party; but rather to deal with any disagreements that arise between us within the relationship itself. Most commonly, this agreement is breached when dissatisfied clients consult another therapist, nominally for a "second opinion", but are actually seeking endorsement of their negative transference towards their present therapist. However, by and large, therapists can rely on the professionalism of their colleagues to refuse this service. I certainly refuse to see anybody currently in a relationship with another therapist without the explicit permission of that therapist to do so.

Realistically, though, I expect and even encourage clients to talk about their therapeutic progress with the intimate others in their lives.

Payment for time

Therapists, like all professionals, should have standard fees for their services. Inevitably, there will be potential clients who claim they cannot afford the fee stated and will ask if a reduction is possible. Individual therapists will decide this issue for themselves, but I recommend that when you are willing to reduce your fee for a particular client, you do so in a way that imposes responsibility on the client, rather than

Rescuing the client with a ready-made "sliding scale". Thus, if you are willing to make a reduction in your fee for a particular client, I recommend you say something along the lines of, "My usual fee is £50 per hour. I am prepared to accept whatever part of that you can afford on a regular basis; and I rely on you to increase your fee as your means allow." The vast majority of clients respond honestly and appreciatively to such a statement. Occasionally, you may be conned, but I believe this is worthwhile in terms of your own observable openness, honesty, and trustworthiness, which will tend to invoke openness, honesty, and trustworthiness in your clients—at least, it is to be hoped, in their relationship to you.

You also need to state the length of time of each session you will have with the client (be it fifty minutes, an hour, or whatever); and you need to stick rigorously to that time. It is neither "generous" nor "kind" to over-run sessions, but rather it is Rescuing behaviour which discomforts the client and lessens his respect for your professionalism.

Whatever the fee agreed, it is important to make clear that the client will have to pay for all sessions agreed to irrespective of absence for any reason. Explain that exceptions to this rule inevitably invoke disputes that may be difficult to resolve. Is 'flu, for example, a justifiable cause of absence, but not a common cold? And what of a "fluey cold"? Most clients understand and accept the legitimate rationale of this ruling, which especially needs to be applied rigidly to members of a therapeutic group in fairness to all the members of that group.

When clients come to you for individual sessions, you may choose to be a bit more liberal, perhaps forgoing fees, at your own discretion, when notice of unavoidable absence is given. But generally speaking, remember the Woody Allen joke in which a client, telling his friend about therapy, says, "If you drop dead of a heart attack, they charge you for the sessions you miss."

Sometimes, clients who can presently not afford your usual fee offer to pay you "later", when they get a rise or their boat comes in, or whatever, or give you their artistic creations or domestic services in lieu of payment. I suggest you refuse such options. I believe it is unfair to impose future indebtedness to you on a client; and the chances are that you will not consider the services or goods he offers in lieu of payment to be of as great a value as your fee.

When I was first a patient in group psychoanalysis, I was poverty-stricken by the fees I was paying to complete my university degree, and my analyst granted me a very reduced fee. Soon after I graduated and got my first job, I offered to increase my payment to my analyst to his full fee plus a bit more in appreciation of his previous generosity to me and the benefit I had so far received from the therapy. He accepted this, which enabled me to feel the pride of responsible grown-upness rather than feeling an indulged but patronised dependent child. Occasionally, in my own practice, a client on reduced fees has behaved similarly towards me, to the gratification of both of us. And to all those clients who express tentativeness about accepting my offer of a reduced fee, I am able to persuade them that I am only returning what I am grateful myself to have been given.

Counselling or therapy

In today's world, where short-term therapy is the norm, the term "therapy" is increasingly abjured in favour of "counselling", even though the training of counsellors is ever more extended. As well as representing the true state of affairs, I believe this change of nomenclature is also a manifestation of contemporary political correctness in which the idea of "therapy" smacks of elitism and unacceptable patronage of the client (who, for similar reasons, is very rarely called a "patient" any longer). But all practitioners need to be aware that there is a true distinction between counselling and therapy that should not be blurred.

Counselling accepts the client's presenting problems at face value; and while it may touch on deeper, underlying issues in the psyche, it rarely, if ever, insists on ignoring the manifest problems in favour of the deeper issues of which the manifest problems are merely symptomatic.

True psychotherapy probes and pummels at the deepest levels of the psyche and, by definition, involving as it does transference and countertransference, takes at least many months and more often years. Practitioners need to communicate with their potential clients these differences and to be aware of the route they are choosing. Often, today, consultations begin as counselling sessions but gradually devolve into full-blown psychotherapy.

Counselling is more pragmatic, has a more *ad hoc* nature, and is easier and more pleasant for both practitioner and client than psychotherapy. Where time and money are limited, counselling is often preferred to psychotherapy, but it is important to bear in mind that there is a distinction between them which deserves not to be overlooked.

Termination of therapy

This is a central issue of the whole therapeutic relationship, although it is often less relevant to counselling.

When a client's deep vulnerabilities are touched in confrontation by the therapist, his normal defence is a desire to terminate the therapy, which he rationalises in any number of ways. This is the time when the therapist's skills are put to their greatest test, and though she will inevitably sometimes fail, it is her prime obligation to put herself and her client through the challenge of bearing and overcoming the client's resistance. When this battle succeeds, the client profoundly appreciates that he stayed the course.

Up until the point of confrontation, psychotherapy can be a pleasant experience for the client, not unlike talking to a sensitive friend; and if the client does leave as soon as the going gets tough, it can be argued that he has wasted the time and money he has so far spent on the therapeutic relationship. And the therapist may be left with a self-demeaning feeling of failure, even though she needs to learn that, as in all creative tasks, being a psychotherapist involves failures along the path to overall success.

In anticipation of the time when confrontation will arise, the therapist needs, in her preliminary interview with the client, to seek his cooperation in advance. I suggest a statement along the following lines: "In the course of your therapy, you are likely to experience times when you will feel acutely uncomfortable and will be prompted to leave. You are likely to give yourself all kinds of reasons for leaving, such as, 'This has been very interesting, but I can't see it going anywhere useful', 'The other people (in the group) have lesser/greater problems than I have', 'I feel completely misunderstood by you (the therapist and/or the other members of the group)'. I need you to trust me that, under no circumstances will I seek to prevent you from leaving therapy when I believe you are ready to do so. I know you are a free agent and may leave therapy whenever you choose, but I ask you to respect my expertise and, whatever your feelings and however great your desire to leave, *you agree to talk through with me (and the group) your desire to leave,* before *you decide to do so*. There is all the difference in the world between 'I want to leave' and 'I've decided to leave'." Even though the client is unlikely to understand the importance of this demand at the beginning of your relationship, it is very useful to be able to recollect and allege it later, when the need arises.

I also recommend contracting with all clients that *after* agreement has been reached that they will shortly terminate their therapy, their termination date be set for (at least) one month hence in order for their relationship to you (and the group, where relevant) to be phased out gently, the t's crossed and the i's dotted, and the opportunity allowed for them to change their minds about leaving (which they sometimes do).

Self-disclosure

How much of herself the therapist discloses to her clients depends largely on her temperamental inclination. I certainly think it behoves every therapist to answer openly and truthfully any initial questions a potential client poses concerning the therapist's qualifications, experience, and general orientation. I, personally, enjoy allowing my clients to experience me as relatively open in my relevant disclosure of my own nature, life, and hang-ups. Most clients seem to like and trust therapists more for their shared humanity; but they quickly show boredom and/or irritation if the therapist goes too far; they are paying for attention to *their* needs, not the therapist's.

In all matters pertaining to being a contemporary psychotherapist, there is an effortful tightrope act to be walked between a large number of polarised dimensions. Traditional psychoanalysts have a much easier job, bound as they are by the rigid rules of their practice that also thoroughly shield them from being "known" by their clients. Those of us who tread the boards in some uncertainty and trepidation perform, I believe, a much more effortful job that is also much more creative and personally gratifying.

Tips and techniques

Explicit and overt therapeutic techniques (such as hypnosis, gestalt two-chair work, visualisation, dramatic role play) should, I believe, be delayed until reliable basic trust has been established between client and therapist. Otherwise, to the client, such techniques may feel like a cold abnegation by the therapist of the warmth of relating in straightforward eye-to-eye dialogue. Nevertheless, there are some devices, supplementary rather than alternative to dialogue, that I have found useful and my clients have appreciated.

Writing and reading notes

Throughout my more than thirty years' practice as a psychotherapist, I have imposed on myself the chore of writing clear notes in coherent sentences (from my Adult ego state) concerning the therapeutic work that was done by each of my clients in each session (be it individual or group). At the beginning of the next session, I read my notes to my clients, very much in the spirit of "minutes of the previous meeting". For clients, this is highly valued as representative of my effort of understanding and interest I have in them.

It also reminds them of details of the previous session that they might have forgotten, and gives them the chance to challenge the accuracy of my reportage, in response to which I may amend my notes. These notes also provide a sense of continuity between one session and the next, and a jumping-off point for a session if there is no other obvious starting point.

My accumulated notes for clients are always available for them to borrow and read at their leisure, and when they leave therapy they take all their notes with them as a record and testament of their tangible achievements.

Mini-contracts

Within the context of long-term (although flexible) contracts for change that clients have in their therapy, I find it useful to establish mini-contracts for each session. These are usually easily articulated by the client in response to my question, at the beginning of the session, "What would you like to achieve in the next hour?" This is also a reminder to the client that she is an autonomous adult, as responsible as I am for what she gets out of the session.

In the context of group therapy, mini-contracts are particularly valuable in ensuring that all members of the group are aware of what each of the others needs and wants from the session; and we have an explicit understanding in my groups that we will all consciously seek to help all members achieve their mini-contracts in the course of the session, although each member is basically responsible for his or her own achievement and has no recourse to complain if their own contract is not achieved. Sometimes, one or more members of the group are beset by critically immediate problems in their lives, and the whole session may be devoted to these, with the unselfish understanding of the rest of the group.

As I go round the room asking each client in turn at the beginning of the session, "What do you want from this session?", an acceptable response is "To be" (which, of course, may prove as profoundly productive a session for that individual as for those who make elaborate statements of intent). Mini-contracts provide the headers for each individual's notes for each session.

Setting homework

Homework tasks, like contracts, demand of the client that she be an active participant in her therapy and turn what can otherwise be an elusively abstract process into a tangible one. Homework—whether behavioural or contemplative—also keeps the client in touch with her therapy between sessions which, these days, are usually spaced by at least a week. Homework set is also recorded in a client's notes, and failure to do it is challenged.

Telephone availability

While it is important strictly to limit any between-session conversations you have with clients on the telephone, I think such availability in the case of a felt pressing need by the client is an expression of appropriate human warmth on the part of the therapist. I make clear that I am generally available for a phone conversation of up to five minutes' duration between sessions, if a special need arises; but if more time is needed, then an additional session needs to be booked.

CHAPTER THREE

Thinking

Theories and languages

Vested interest

A psychological theory tends to define its adherents as vehement enemies of the adherents of any other psychological theory. Certainly, there are factions within other disciplines, but less often than in psychology do theoretical differences exert a powerful enough divisive influence to compete with the natural sympathy between people of similar interests. Thus it is clear that psychologists of whichever (Parent) school often have very strong (Child) investments in their chosen profession, and tend hotly to defend the professed superiority of their own chosen orientation. Of course, we all claim our own theories are the closest match to objective (Adult) reality.

Environmental influences

More positively, different theories may be thought of as different but concordant languages. Within very broad limits, any language is capable of expressing any thought that any human being may wish to utter. From China to the Azores, we are all one species. However, environmental conditions, both physical and psychological, have created differences in the relative importance and pertinence of various elements in different peoples' experiences of life. And these differences are reflected in the vocabulary of any given culture-language. A centrally important issue will have invoked the creation of minutely discriminating words to match the need to perceive such difference. Thus, we are told the Inuit have many words for our one word "snow"; and the few words of Yiddish I know enable me to describe varieties of fools with subtlety and gusto.

Multi-lingualism

The vast majority of contemporary therapeutically oriented psychological theories are extensions and elaborations of psychoanalysis into the realm of the ego. Differences are essentially of focus.

In his emphasis on the universal unconscious, timeless conflict between the id and the superego, Freud left the tiny part in each of our egos that is capable of objectivity and autonomy largely uncharted. The ego, as a whole, he considered basically in terms of its *defence mechanisms*, which serve to shield the individual from being overwhelmed by the otherwise unmanageable forces of the superego and the id. And notwithstanding their being defined structurally as part of the ego, defence mechanisms are largely unconscious. The autonomous, conscious self in whose existence we take such pride is but a minute portion of the ego which, in turn, is but a fraction of our wholeness.

But despite its anatomical minuteness, it is only by means of this reflective, objective part of us that we have any hope of directing ourselves towards increasing contentment. With this goal in mind, post-Freudian humanistic psychology has taken up the task of elaborating the nature of the autonomous part of the ego.

All useful psychological theories comprehensively account for the ways in which all human beings are alike and the ways in which they differ. Each theory describes our wholeness and dissects that wholeness in its own way, thus revealing a particular cross-section. When we are observing a particular fact about any individual, its best fit is sometimes most vividly displayed in the context of one theory rather than another. Thus, while we will each inevitably be most fluent in our theoretical native tongue, a degree of multi-lingualism can do nothing but enrich our experience and our expressiveness. In my own practice as a psychotherapist, Transactional Analysis is my native tongue, which serves me very well. But there are occasions when my limited vocabulary in a number of other theories enables me spontaneously to add moments of extra vividness to my perceptions. I highly recommend any practitioner to do likewise, viewing different languages as parallel, equally valid holistic conceptualisations, rather than in combat with each other, competing for "rightness".

Conversely, in so far as we are all holograms, we may creatively and inductively develop our own theories. Given sufficient attention, any part of us can be seen to be representative of our wholeness. Palmistry, iridology, graphology, physiognomy, reflexology, homeopathy, acupuncture, blood groupings, astrological sun signs, racial stereotypes, biochemistry, anatomical types, bio-energetics, Enneagram types … all bear witness—some more successfully than others—to our instinctive appreciation of our holographic nature. All that is required is a prolonged, fascinated, obsessive concentration on some sign from which we can eventually evolve a coherent theory. A four-foot-six-inch-tall man who was also, briefly, something of a television celebrity avowed he had constructed a reliable personality typology out of his perception of the shapes of people's nostrils! (My own typology, obsessively pursued and developed for twenty years from within the framework of Transactional Analysis, is outlined in the next chapter of this book).

Body and mind and nature and nurture are inextricably entwined as the determinants of our achieved wholeness, which all theories seek to understand and dissect.

Humanistic-existential assumptions

Conditioning

We infer that, to the newborn baby, itself and the universe are a buzzing, whirring, inchoate oneness, associated with which is the infant's utter vulnerability and lack of self-sufficiency. But happily our brains are hard-wired to rapidly make sense of both the physical and psychological worlds into which we are thrust.

Making sense of the world and of people is the means by which we are enabled to make the impact between ourselves and physical reality and between ourselves and other people *predictable*. So, out of our earliest experiences, we construct virtually inviolable *theories* that serve our core needs to stay alive and get what we want in the face of the infinite number of stimuli that bombard us.

Once having formulated our theories, our minds thereafter filter out the information received by our sense organs that is irrelevant to or contradicts those theories. By about the age of six, to all intents and purposes, our minds are closed, and nearly every experience we subsequently allow ourselves to have is a recapitulation, literally or metaphorically, of evidence of the truths we have established.

All sane people within a culture share more or less congruent theories about physical reality. True, an artist may see "nothing but" colours and shapes, a banker will focus on the economic aspects of reality, and a naturalist may find city streets "empty"; but we all respect the law of gravity, know the dangers of cars and fires, that yellow and blue make green … and a thousand other facts.

I remember one of my daughters, then aged four, asking me, "Mummy, why are all the big aeroplanes at the airport and all the little ones in the sky?", to which I was obliged—in the name of sanity—to reply, "The o nes in the sky are really big, too. They just look little because they are a long way away." I recall feeling some poignancy that, in my reply, I was closing my daughter's mind to all other metaphysical possibilities in which, for example, the aeroplanes at the airport could be deemed to be *really* little, but only look big because they are so close. (Fortunately, our minds do not become completely closed, as witnessed by the existence of creative thinkers of all kinds, who dare us to re-open our minds to the frightening but exciting possibilities we last experienced in early childhood).

In the same way, and in order to fulfil the same basic need to make sense of the world so as to feel *secure* in it, we learn about psychological reality. Learning about physical reality enables us safely and confidently to interact with *things*; learning about psychological reality enables us safely and confidently to interact with *people*. Making sense of people means learning how to give and get strokes.

All the time we are asking our mothers and fathers about gravity and temperature, animals and birds, night and day, sand and snow … and about a thousand and one other physical realities that impinge on us, we are also asking about men and women, life and death, love and hate, anger, jealousy, ownership rights and sharing, happiness and unhappiness, good and bad, reward and punishment, and so on. And so, by the time we first leave home to go to school, we are basically equipped to get our stroke needs met in the world at large.

However, we all make one huge mistake—a mistake that most people continue to make for the rest of their lives. We presume that just because everybody else's physical reality is more or less the same as ours, so everybody else's psychological reality is also very like our own. It isn't.

True, there are large areas of overlap between one person's and another's psychological realities, or else we would all continually fail to get strokes from other people. But the unavoidable truth—which accounts for the vast bulk of our experienced emotional pains—is that each person's stroke needs and learned ways of getting their stroke needs met are to a large extent idiosyncratic. In contradistinction to our largely shared conditioning about physical reality, what we witnessed, experienced, and were told about people in our early family life may be vastly different from the conditioning of many others we encounter.

In this way, one child becomes the man whose greatest happiness is his close and loving family life, his greatest difficulty in life being his constant worry about money. Another becomes renowned in his field of work and feels immensely rewarded by the honours heaped on him but constantly does battle with his alcoholism. One woman is constantly appreciated for her femininity and beauty but feels inferior for never having completed her secondary schooling, while another is profoundly positively stroked as a mother but is miserable as a wife.

Thus, for the good and bad in our lives, what is *relevant* to one person is *irrelevant* to another. Wealth versus poverty, health versus illness, fame versus anonymity, faith versus doubt, intelligence versus stupidity, beauty versus ugliness, security versus adventure are some of the most common dimensions to be found in people's psychological structures.

Discovering the dimensions that are relevant to a particular person is revealing the nature of that person at the profoundest level. A superficially trivial experience in one of my therapy groups some years ago was extremely educative in this regard. One evening, around December the twentieth, as I entered my living room to conduct a group therapy session, with all the members of the group already present, I overheard one group member saying to another, "Thank you for your Christmas card. I'm sorry I haven't sent any this year. I hope you don't think I'm ungrateful." The word "ungrateful" sounded to me a bit odd in the context, until I apprehended that the woman who uttered it was experiencing and referring to her own *target negative stroke*. So I stopped in my tracks and asked all the other members of the group quickly and spontaneously to declare how they would feel, encountering a friend just before Christmas from whom they had received an unreciprocated Christmas card. The responses included "guilty", "embarrassed", "ashamed", "stupid", and—believe it or not—"triumphant". What was most salutary was that, as each person uttered his or her own target negative stroke, others looked on in amazed disbelief. Finally, one of the "guilty" ones turned to the one who originally expressed her ingratitude and said, "But you do feel guilty *for* being ungrateful, don't you?", to which the "ungrateful" one replied, "No".

It was like a controlled experiment. That is, keeping the circumstance trivial and constant, from which people's negative target strokes were elicited, forced them all to acknowledge the subjective nature of their differing realities. Had the chosen experience been more significantly distressing or one that not everybody had at some time suffered, the group members would have been able to rationalise their differences as, "But we really all feel the same".

Fate and free will

The problem of free will has always been available for the pleasure of mental masochists. It cannot be solved, only dissolved.

By definition, the human brain is capable of comprehending only that which is less complex than itself; and, by definition, our concept of fate refers to a meaning more complex than we can apprehend, emanating as it does from a source whose power is greater than our own. We can only dissolve the problem pragmatically by living at the highest level of free will available to us while accepting, from the evidence, that there are bound to be times in our lives when a higher consciousness than we are capable of seems to mock our lower-level morality and purpose.

Humanistic psychology understands that although the conditions and experiences that were imposed on us in early childhood were significantly instrumental in propelling us towards the existential conclusions at which we arrived, we are held responsible for our interpretations of those experiences. Perhaps our genetically determined predispositions prompted us to the particular sense we made of our experiences; witness the often very disparate interpretations siblings have of their shared experiences. But by whatever combination of nature and nurture we rationalise and justify our perceptions of the world and other people, there are always conclusions other than the ones we arrived at that would equally fit the data imposed on us. Notwithstanding that throughout our lives we are tightly constrained to respond in accordance with our earliest conditioning, we have some wriggling room within our chains and our cages.

Furthermore, from the vantage point of our grown-up selves, our earliest existential decisions can be seen often to be naively plausible but mistaken. I remember a woman in one of my therapy groups who was struggling to revive and maintain her marriage. One evening, as she was leaving home to come to the group, her four-year-old son asked her why she was going out. She replied, "I've got to go and talk to some people so we can live with Daddy." The next morning, when she got up, she found her son had got up earlier and wreaked havoc in their living room, upturning furniture and pulling all the books off their shelves. He continued to behave with violent distress for a number of days, to his mother's total incomprehension. In the group, we struggled to understand what had precipitated this deep disturbance in the child. Eventually, we comprehended, with the aid of the mother's questioning of her son, that when she had said to him, "I've got to go and talk to some people so we can live with Daddy", he had understood that if she didn't come to the group, she and he would die!

Undoubtedly, whether we remember them or not, whether they are trivial or profoundly consequential, each of us has a collection of interpretations in our minds based on the extreme literalness with which we first understood language.

Our grown-up minds are nearly, but not quite, closed. First, facts incompatible with our beliefs may insistently refuse to go away. Occasionally in human history, an Einstein challenges a Newton and, despite our denials, ridicule, and inquisitions, when its time has come, the new idea will be heard, and reality is extended or transformed to accommodate it. Individuals, too, may rarely have mind-blowing experiences—usually profoundly traumatic—that permanently alter their deepest theories of reality.

Second, we all desire to experience again the excitement of our earliest years before we had yet chosen the life-preserving truths we would live by. For this, we flirt with death—physically or mentally—from the thrills of rock climbing, motor racing, or riding the big dipper, to courses in philosophy that challenge us to realise that all knowledge and beliefs are tenuous and ultimately unproven.

But in accordance with the decisions we made in early childhood we all go on seeking, and finding, the same strokes—positive as well as negative—over and over again. Actually changing the handful of existential decisions that constitute the core of our being is radical surgery of the soul, requiring prolonged psychotherapy; but there are many much easier ways of increasing our overall wellbeing without resort to such drastic measures. Even some of the most horrible decisions can be twisted to find positive fulfilment. A profoundly unhappy heroin addict who once consulted me disclosed that he was living by a core decision that "Life is waiting for death". Notwithstanding his utter misery and futility, he found some small degree of pleasure in life through the part-time job he had working in a morgue!

Caged as we are, we are always free to make the most and the best rather than the least and the worst of our decisions and to paint the bars of our cages in colours of our choice.

Life as faction

We create the world with our thoughts. Out of the amorphous clay of the universe in which we exist, we sculpt the forms that give our lives meaning: experiences, ideas, and "other people" that are joyful and painful, beautiful and ugly, good and evil. We are all inventions of each other. Because we are human, we are glad to accept responsibility for the joy and beauty and good in our lives, but prefer to perceive the pain and ugliness and bad in our lives as fortuitously happening to us or involuntarily imposed on us by other people.

As grown-ups, our narcissism hides itself in webs of camouflage that we sophisticatedly spin, but our primary aim in every instance of pain, ugliness, or evil in which we participate is to maintain the perception of our own righteousness. "It's your fault" projection begins as soon as we have developed a clear concept of our own self and equivalent selves in others—certainly by about age three—which is the baseline on which we build the edifices of our egos. *In extremis*, when the attacks of others are more than our projective defences can withstand, our egos regress to the most primitive level of consciousness in which it is still possible to maintain a sense of self; other selves cease to exist, and we are left with our single self, distinct only from the rest of the universe, against which we flailingly deny our responsibility with "I didn't do it". However we have orchestrated our themes in our earliest months and years of life, we are bound to them. We can never fully escape the dimensions we created for ourselves in childhood, but the possibilities we can choose within them are hugely various.

Diagnosis

At every moment of our lives, our overall response to our situation and to other people is informed by three contexts: the unchanging attributes of our humanity, our individuality, and our present stage of development in life. The relative influence of each of these contexts at a given moment may vary, although, broadly speaking, our "stage of development" tends to predominate in childhood, our individuality in our middle years, and, ideally, as we grow old, the spirituality associated with our humanity, especially in our coming to terms with ageing and death.

In our humanity, we are all the same in being united in our lifelong concerns with pain and death, good versus evil, conflicting quests for excitement and security, and the overall quest for meaning in our lives. These are constant dynamic components of our minds that we need to be implicitly aware of as constants in every consideration of any human being.

The whole picture

There is no such thing as a single or correct definition of a house or a horse, let alone of a human being.

Everything depends on the frame of reference used. Some popular frames of reference used by human beings to define themselves and other things are mathematics, physics, chemistry, biology, philosophy, psychology, anthropology, sociology, political theory, history, economics, religion, cosmology, art, drama, music, and poetry. The number of "facts" from which meaning may be extracted is infinite, so the choice of frame of reference for any particular person depends on a judgement (made by Parent and Adult collaboration) concerning which synoptic view focuses with greatest clarity on those facts we deem to have greatest significance. To find out even one thing necessarily involves ignoring or devaluing something else.

The most satisfying revelations are usually made when we see the meaning of a fact within two or more frames of reference at the same time. When validated by the Adult in each of the separate frames of reference, this then becomes what we recognise as an original thought.

Life is movement towards the wholeness of the picture we want to see in the end. When the picture is complete, we are ready to die. If we merely allow our picture to put itself together, our lives are safe and dull and passionless; if we create our pictures as artists, we are never sure what exactly our completed picture will look like, and our lives are uncertain and exciting. Life is the opposite of certainty; but so is chaotic uncertainty the opposite of art. Striving for the optimal balance between order and chaos, rest and busyness, the fear of death and the quest for excitement, discipline and spontaneity—is the volatile, unremitting quest of the whole of our lives, whether we are conscious of it or not.

We create our lives retrospectively, when a certain distance enables us to see episodes of the past as distinct pieces of the jigsaw puzzle we are putting together to make the picture of our lives. A completed patch of our jigsaw puzzle may give us enough to guess, by extrapolation, what the whole picture is about, but we may have to change our minds as we proceed. We make mistakes when we try to squeeze the wrong piece of experience or the wrong person into a particular place, and the artist in us is then ashamed and seeks to negate our folly.

We are all inventions of each other, and we re-create the world with our thoughts, for as long as we are alive.

Categorising

There is no such thing as a neutral or motive-free observation. Our frames of reference provide the categories into which we sort the data, and these influence our perception in two ways: first, we ignore the data that do not fit any of our categories; and second, we probe for data to fill as many as possible of the categories of our frame of reference, in order to make our perception comprehensive.

Concerning our individuality, categorising is the primary function of the human brain in making sense of anything and everything. Human vanity is piqued by this fact because it reduces the significance of the exceptional characteristics of ourselves in which most people take such pride. But, outside our essentially narcissistic frame of reference, the two most interesting observations that can be made about people are always their differences and their samenesses. Male or female is the first and most wide-ranging categorisation of any person that we all immediately make. "It's a girl" or "It's a boy" is the first observation ever made about any human being, and a very large number of other dichotomous characterisations by which we describe people, concepts, and the inanimate world can readily be seen to be closely derived from the basic category of gender.

Some categorisations of people and ideas and things are discrete, and some are sub-sets of wider categorisations we have already made. Which discrete categories we apply and how far we go in refining any of our categorisation by such sub-categories depends on the context in which the person, idea, or thing is being described. "Men" is sufficient in the context of public lavatories; "female, 5'6", aged 22, 38–24–36" is sufficient in a beauty contest; and "intelligent, moderate socialist" may be sufficient for a trade-union election. So it goes on, to the limiting case of a beloved other whom we wish to describe, and thus know, down to the tiniest freckle of his or her physical and psychological being.

In the context of psychology, a sufficient description of a person requires categorisation of him or her in terms of a defined number of ways in which individuals express the motivations common to all human beings. A good-enough theory of personality will justify the categories it uses as being comprehensive in relation to its assumptions about human nature; and it will also offer some rationalisations of why individuals differ from each other.

Categorising ourselves and others psychologically by means of theories that are appropriately deep and comprehensive enlarges our awareness of the samenesses and differences between people, adding a dimension of objective understanding to our emotional reactions to events and to other people. It is commonly received wisdom that, in judging others, the more like us they are, the more accurate our assessment of them is likely to be; and unless we categorise people psychologically, we implicitly take all of our own characteristics to be the human norm, and we discount the validity of all the characteristics of other people except those that are also our own. And understanding the dynamic meaning of our own type in relation to the known type of another individual enables us to please that individual with finesse, if we so desire, and most effectively defend our vulnerabilities against the assaults of that individual, if the need arises. Categorising people psychologically enlarges our humanity and increases our tolerance of ourselves as well as others. For the price of forgoing some of our narcissistic allegiance to our intrinsic uniqueness, we gain a corresponding diminishment of shame for our shortcomings, which we can now accept as "only human".

As well as categorising ourselves and others in terms of our individuality, we also validly categorise ourselves and others in terms of the characteristics associated with our ages. This can be very important in the context of psychotherapeutic diagnosis where, for example, the fact of stealing by a fourteen-year-old boy may be relatively insignificant, but not so in the case of an eight-year-old; and school phobia in a five-year-old may be presumed, in the first instance, to be normal and transient, but not so in a thirteen-year-old.

Under the age of three, the child is primarily concerned with coming to terms with and making sense of physical reality. In the Oedipal stage, between three and six, the child is coming to terms with and making sense of emotional reality. In latency, between about six and twelve, the child is coming to terms with the reality of death, acquiring basic literacy and numeracy, and becoming socially competent, especially amongst his or her same-sexed peers.

At puberty, we are overwhelmed by our sexual urges together with our ambivalent dependency needs and desire to be self-sufficient and autonomous. In late adolescence, we polish up our Parent ego state through combative intellectual discourse with our parents, in preparation for leaving home and becoming self-sufficient in the adult world.

In our twenties, we tend either to settle down into grown-up responsibilities or else sow our wild oats; and around twenty-nine to thirty, we redress the balance of freedom and responsibility in our lives.

In our thirties, we usually pursue our worldly goals and ambitions with enthusiasm, only to come up against the "mid-life crisis" of our forties, when our earlier enthusiasms have palled, our lives feel stale, and we seek the excitement of radical newness and adventure "before it is too late".

In our fifties, we become aware that the era of our achievement in the wider world is nearly over. For many parents, this is the time when the last of their children are leaving home, and mothers in particular feel bereft of the core significance that rearing their children has given to their lives. New interests and goals need to be developed to give meaning to the many years of life still left.

In our sixties, retirement from paid employment looms, and men in particular need to find meaning in their lives beyond their role as breadwinners. Women feel their domestic domain intruded on by their retired husbands and bemoan, with Dorothy Parker, "I know I married him for better or for worse, but not for lunch."

At seventy, we are all aware that our three-score-years-and-ten are up and continued life is a bonus. This is the time when people seek to put their worldly affairs in order in readiness for death. But for many, this is a time when there is also a sense that our duties are finished and, with whatever life is left to us, we are entitled to do our own thing, untrammelled by any Adapted Child "oughts".

In our eighties and beyond, ideally, the whole of our lives can be surveyed with wisdom and detachment, and we are able to withdraw from mundane concerns into a serene, mystical transcendence of our ego and all its fears and strivings, coming full circle back to our one-ness with the universe in which we began our lives.

Translating metaphors

Humans are metaphorical beings, and all languages are full of universally understood metaphors which express wisdom accumulated by mankind over aeons of time. Language itself may be thought of as the ulti-mate metaphor for experience. Some of our deepest individual truths are discoverable through universal metaphors, and many metaphors do us the service of counterbalancing much unwisdom contained in the often invalid dichotomy of mind–body. Thus I remem-ber a new member of one of my therapy groups telling us, "I always feel I should swallow my bad feelings", and I asked, "Do you get indigestion?" She replied, "Oh yes, I've always suffered terrible indigestion." The rest of the group smiled in recognition of the holistic truth she had just expressed about herself, but she herself needed to have explained the significance of her answer as well as how I had come to ask the question. It is at this point that diagnosis blends into therapy, since the revelatory "*I never thought of it that way before*" in itself often provides much relief from dis-ease. Freely mixing and generally playing with metaphors in the context of therapy is, for me, the single most enjoyable and powerful technique associated with both diagnosis and therapy.

It is strangely true that what we remember being told about our births, or facts associated with our births, are precise metaphors for our relationships to other people. Since what we remember being told does not always correspond to the independent testimony of our parents, it seems we create our stories to match our achieved ways of experiencing others.

"I know nothing about my birth" probably means "I have no understanding of how I relate to other people". "I/my mother nearly died" probably means "I/other people experience great distress in my relationships to them". One woman told me, "When she was pregnant with me, my mother could eat hardly any foods, but the few she could eat she loved". This was confirmed to mean, "I don't like most people, but I have a few very loving relationships". And a paranoic schizophrenic told me, "When I was born, they held me upside-down and I cried and they laughed"!

Other easily translated metaphors that probe even more deeply into our existential frames of reference can be revealed by answers to four simple questions. Reveal yourself to yourself by answering these questions before reading the interpretative key below them.

1. In a few words, describe your favourite animal (or bird or fish).
2. In a few words, describe your second favourite animal (or bird or fish).
3. In a few words, describe the sun.
4. In a few words, describe the sea.

1) reveals our self-perception; 2) reveals our ego-ideal and the kind of people we are drawn to love; 3) reveals our present and/or childhood experience of home; 4) reveals our truth about sex.

The beauty of these questions is that they can be asked without impropriety, and answered without embarrassment, between complete strangers as well as intimates, yet they provide, in a jiffy, deeply useful knowledge of any person and the potential for a relationship between people.

Some memorable answers I have received to these questions include: a bisexual man for whom the sea is "variable"; a man whose favourite creature was a cat and whose second favourite was a budgerigar; and a lesbian woman whose favourite animal was a cat and whose response to the question of her second favourite creature was, "I can only think of a cat".

Another universally true metaphorical equivalence in our lives is that of time and money. Time and its flow, from the known past through ungraspable present to indeterminate future, is a pervasive reality woven into the fabric of our consciousness. Money, too (or its bartering equivalent), is an invention necessary in our quotidian lives, and each individual, in his or her idiosyncratic way, construes and relates to money in exactly the same way as he or she does to time.

We *spend* both time and money. Paradoxically, we are happiest when we are least aware of them. Our experience of having more than enough as well as less than enough of either or both of them disturbs our equanimity. Optimally, we have enough of each to meet our survival needs and a little bit extra to play with.

Out of my clinical experience, I have discovered that there are five broad, discrete ways in which people apprehend and spend time and money:

making time and money
using time and money
passing time and frittering money
wasting time and money
killing time and losing money.

While these are specific manifestations of five deep existential decisions by which people live their lives (which will be put in context in Chapter Four) and, as such, contain an element of immutability, I have noticed that people can and do, to some extent, modify their general orientations to time and money and also transiently move amongst the five options according to their present state of wellbeing or dis-ease. Observable changes in a client's orientation to time and money are useful signs of changes taking place in them in the course of therapy.

Basic data

We obtain the data we are seeking, to make our diagnoses, by asking questions of our clients. There is nothing more loving than asking questions of another human being. One useful question to begin with is the open-ended one, "Tell me about yourself".

While the usual most productive way to proceed is with an optimally open mind, responding to the client's disclosures with questions that gradually home in on her unique realities, there are some general facts that may be profoundly revealing, so are worth discovering at the first meeting. Whenever these facts are normative, they may be forgotten, but when they are abnormal, they may enable you very rapidly to infer some core existential dimensions of your client that might otherwise not be uncovered for a long time. As a matter of course, I ask all my new clients: How old are you?; Are your parents alive? (If not, when and how did they die?); Are your parents living together? (If not, how did they come to separate, and how old were you at that time?); Do you have any step-parents?; How many brothers and sisters do you have, and what is your position in the family? (Apart from gender and genetics in general, birth order is known to be the most influential factor in determining an individual's personality.) Are you married? divorced? in a long-term intimate relationship? Do you have children? (If so, how old are they, and what are their names?) What is your occupation, and do you like it?

Often, most of the answers you receive to these questions will be normative, but it is the singularities in your client you are seeking. Never neglect the possibility that one or more of the answers to the above questions sum up the most important issue(s) the client needs to face.

Therapy

What is therapy?

Therapy is helping people find out what they want and then helping them to get it. The former task is almost always by far the more prolonged. Finding out what people want involves discovering the *meanings* of their symptoms—symptoms being both bodily and psychological. The pursuit of meanings involves microscopic analysis, that is, what in everyday life would be called making mountains out of molehills. Thus therapy is, in large measure, the continuing refinement of diagnosis. Revelation is the goal.

It is important to remember that the symptom is not the disease. In observing a man to be limping, we cannot know without enquiry whether he is limping because he has pins and needles, has one leg shorter than the other, has had a stroke … "Big" symptoms may be of a minor problem; "small" symptoms may be of a major problem.

Once people know what they want, therapy becomes oriented to the behaviour modification necessary to fulfil their wants. Traditional psychoanalysis stops when revelation is considered complete. Purely behavioural therapies discount the necessity of revelation. The vast majority of humanistic-existential therapies pursue meaning and adaptive behavioural change hand in hand.

Any therapy that recognises the centrality of meaning is more art than science. Highly personal validity rather than publicly demonstrable reliability is the measure of therapeutic success. Accuracy rather than precision is the target, since qualitative as well as quantitative truths can be accurate, whereas precision refers to measurable exactitude—which is irrelevant to subjective reality. (Furthermore, even when exactitude is relevant, a high degree of precision is spurious and misleading if accuracy is lacking. For example, no matter that a micrometer screw gauge measures to within one-thousandth of an inch if, unbeknown to the experimenter, the screw gauge itself is warped.) The criterion of repeatability which would gain therapy the status of "science" is impossible to achieve because each human being is unique.

The variety of humanistic therapies

All therapies assume that the conditioning of the individual in infancy and early childhood is an important determiner of the individual's lifelong propensities to respond to life in the ways he or she does. And all therapies assume the necessity for—one way or another—undoing faulty conditioning. All therapies also propound—at least implicitly—principles of conservation and flow of energy. Somewhere in every therapy is the notion of energy flowing freely in health and being blocked in pathology. As functional beings, humans are likened to the rest of the universe. These assumptions are the heritage of Freud.

There is now a vast array of humanistic therapies for the practitioner to choose amongst. Some abjure the touching of the client by the therapist and so are strictly verbal; others value highly the beneficial effects of (literal) stroking; others do both in about equal measure. But the vast majority of contemporary therapies are built on the foundation of psychoanalysis and, theoretically, are elaborations of the psychoanalytic ego. Each therapist chooses his or her primary therapeutic modality according to his or her temperament and taste.

Anxiety and depression

Anxiety and depression underlie all psychopathology. They are polarised opposites in the human psyche but are equally distressing. All human beings naturally experience either or both from time to time in reactive response to the contingencies of life that befall them; but anybody who has experienced either condition in an acute and/or prolonged form can testify to the overwhelming pain and dysfunction associated with them. All mundane concerns become meaningless, and the sufferer struggles very hard to be willing to stay alive.

Anxiety and depression refer to the pre-three-year-old stage of human development, at which time we are all forced to come to terms with *existence itself*, which is the necessary precursor of our coming to terms with the demands of relating to others. The adult sufferer has inevitably regressed to his pre-social level of functioning and must be nourished through this stage before any less infantile behaviour is demanded of him.

The experience of anxiety is of being pursued by a lion—all the time. The sufferer is continuously on the run, but the lion keeps chasing him, and he runs faster and faster to the limit of his capacity, until death is longed for as the only way to achieve fearless quietude. The pain is likened to a knife being twisted in one's guts.

The experience of depression is of personal worthlessness. The sufferer is overwhelmed by her unfulfilled narcissistic needs, her movement atrophied to the point of paralysis. Nothing offered her is sufficient to convince her that her life has any value or that she has any hope of finding pleasure in being alive, although she is also terrified of death. The pain is likened to a vast space inside her body that should be filled with the love of which she is unworthy.

Thus the task of the psychotherapist in treating a sufferer of acute and/or prolonged anxiety or depression is an onerous one, closely imitating the unremitting containment and love that a good mother offers her infant. Thank heavens for the drugs than can mitigate the pain; and I profoundly challenge the right of any purist therapist to demand of the patient that she decline to take ameliorative drugs in the name of accessing the meaning of her pain in an uncamouflaged way. But once the symptomatic pain has been sufficiently mitigated, the therapist has the task of dragging the patient, kicking and screaming, out of her existential total self-absorption into the ordinary world of pleasure and meaning as well as pain, associated with interacting with other people. The anxious patient needs to be trained and coerced in obsessiveness, structuring his daily life with the security of containment that comes from order and ritual. And the depressed patient needs to be trained in spontaneous adventurousness, caring for the needs of others, and *acting in the world*, irrespective of life's ultimate meaninglessness.

Needless to say, severely anxious and depressed patients are high suicide risks, and it is a good idea to make "no-suicide contracts" with them—something along the lines of, "In order for me to work with you, I need you to agree that you will not, by accident or on purpose, harm yourself while you are in therapy with me." Perhaps surprisingly, people rarely agree to this contract unless they intend to abide by it, and they are deeply reassured by the containment it offers them. Another useful response to a patient's threat of suicide is, "I can't help you if you're dead".

Stages of therapy

Many clients, in their initial consultation with a therapist ask, "How long will it take?". While, of course, there is no definitive answer to this question, it is generally the case that deeply transformative work cannot be achieved in less than a year or two of weekly therapy sessions.

The first stage of therapy is the establishment of trust. The client needs to feel that she has found a new friend, one who understands her, approves of her, and empathises with her fully. At this stage, the therapist knows—but the client probably does not—that this stage is only the foundation on which true therapy is built.

The second and most prolonged stage of therapy is that of confrontation by the therapist of the client's responsibility for the pains she repetitively experiences in her life. This involves disclosing the client's existential decisions and helping her find ways of making the most and the best rather than the least and the worst of them, by stretching the boundaries of her reality. Most radically, when the client's existential decisions are profoundly self-destructive, an attempt may be made to get the client to disavow one or more of them, although it should always be remembered that to do this is equivalent, for the client, of disavowing gravity, and, if it ever does succeed, will take a very long time.

Therapy is complete when the agreed contract for change in the client is achieved. Rarely is termination fully and mutually satisfactory. External contingencies of many kinds may bring the therapeutic relationship to a premature conclusion, including the common ones of the relocation of the client or therapist. But also, despite the therapist's best efforts, many clients pre-emptively decide to terminate therapy while they are in the midst of some critical resistance and/or have developed a negative transference to the therapist. I recommend that the therapist's response to a client's insistent termination be one by which the door is left open for the client to return later. Nevertheless, it seems to me to be of paramount importance that the therapist, one way or another, demands that the client acknowledge her responsibility for breaking her original agreement (when embarking on the therapy) to act in accordance with trust in the therapist's judgement.

CHAPTER FOUR

Five personality types

The nature of personality

Soon after I started practising as a psychotherapist, I began to notice that certain words, attitudes, feelings, and bodily behaviours in individuals seemed to form clusters. Gradually, over the course of the next twenty years, I inductively developed my observations into a comprehensive theory of five basic personality types, each with its own special handicaps and talents reflecting its own *fundamental existential decision*. I also noticed that these five personality types were, metaphorically, the atoms of which all our egos are constituted. *We are all alike in having all five types in our natures; we are different from each other in the relative strengths and the hierarchical organisation of the types in our individual personalities.*

The five basic types are: the Perfectionist, the Hurrier, the Doormat, the Try Harder, and the Stiff Upper Lipper. The Perfectionist and the Hurrier are concerned with the ways in which we come to terms with existence itself in the first three years of our lives. The Doormat, the Try Harder, and the Stiff Upper Lipper are concerned with the ways in which we come to terms with relating to other people in the Oedipal stage of our development during the second three years of our lives. All of the types are the means by which we defend our fragile egos against the disintegrative forces that threaten them. Similarly to our language ability, we probably have a hard-wired propensity to express all of the five basic personality types, but we require appropriate stimulation in our formative years in order for them to be fully activated. The particularities of each individual's early childhood experiences determine the relative strengths of the five types in his or her personality.

The verbal, attitudinal, and body-language symptoms indicating that people are presently *in* one or other of the (Adapted Child) personality syndromes are not equally reliable. Some signs are common to more than one type, and it is only when a deepest-level existential decision is expressed that we can be sure of which personality type we are observing. Nevertheless, some words, behaviours, attitudes, and facts of life are extremely reliable indicators of one or other of the types, which indicators are given in the table below.

Some typical and very reliable indicators of the five personality types.

Personality type	Words	Non-verbal signs	Facts of life
The Perfectionist	"perfect" "for my sins" "thank God" "absolutely"	pursing of bottom lip between forefinger and thumb, itemising points while speaking	having (even one) Roman Catholic or Jewish parent

(*Continued*)

Table (*Continued*).

The Hurrier	"hurry up!" "futile" "pointless"	being regularly late, noticeable vertical frown marks between eyes	having been to boarding school, having been separated from mother before the age of three
The Doormat	"y'know", "embarrassed" "I know you think that …" "Really?"	hero-worshipping opposite-sexed parent, questioning expression with noticeable horizontal lines on forehead, running fingers through hair	being an only child or more than six years apart from nearest sibling, the premature death of the opposite-sexed parent
The Try Harder	"try", "superior/inferior", "lucky/unlucky", "I envy/admire"	hero-worshipping same-sexed parent, sitting forward with chin in hands and a concentrated and puzzled look	the premature death of the same-sexed parent
The Stiff Upper Lipper	"one" (instead of "I"), "bored", "weak/strong"	(man) having a moustache, pulling socks up	having been to boarding school

Notwithstanding that our lifelong personalities are more or less fully established by the age of about six, we still have to traverse latency, puberty, and adolescence before we reach maturity, and these developmental stages are associated with surges of different personality types, irrespective of individuality. Latency is particularly associated with a Perfectionist defence, puberty with a Hurrier defence, and later adolescence with a Try Harder defence.

In so far as the five personality types are the adaptive structures we have created to defend our egos against their vulnerabilities in relation to the assaults we experience from physical and emotional realities, they are all part of the Adapted Child. Our total egos consist of our Parent, Adult, and Free Child as well as our Adapted Child, but our lives are dominated by our Adapted Childs. My estimate is that in ninety per cent of our functioning we are either wholly in our Adapted Child or in another ego state contaminated by it. Our Free Child is our temperament; the Free Child and Adapted Child combined form the whole of our Child, which is our personality. Our Adult is our truly objective rationality, and our Parent is our character. All of our neurotic pains and our triumphs over them are the stuff of our Adapted Child.

In the final years of my development of my theory, I began to wonder why it is that most people's individual personalities seem to be dominated by *two* of the five basic types, and I eventually realised that this reflects an innate biological-psychological constituent of our human nature, namely the pull of opposite impulses and attitudes and our struggle to reconcile these opposites. Any two of the five basic personality syndromes will have some characteristic in which they are opposite to each other and some characteristic that they share.

Thus a pair of types that is dominant in an individual's personality is a manifestation of both his deepest existential conflict *and* the means by which he seeks—with varying degrees of success—to reconcile these opposites in a satisfying expression of both of them. The table below lists the names I have given to the ten compound personality types, the struggle of opposites, and the reconciling commonalities between them.

Compound personality types.

Basic types	Combined personality	Opposite-ness	Sameness
Perfectionist/ Hurrier	The Uncommitted Doubter/ Passionate Philosopher	fear of death versus fear of life	anxiety
Perfectionist/ Doormat	The Righteous Blamer/ Responsible Leader	absolute versus relative standards of righteousness	moral control and righteousness
Perfectionist/ Try Harder	The Fighter of Lost Causes/ Committed Champion	superiority versus inferiority	intellectual rightness
Perfectionist/ Stiff Upper Lipper	The Cold Intellectual/ Independent Thinker	emotional intensity versus detachment	rationality

(Continued)

Table (*Continued*).

Basic types	Combined personality	Opposite-ness	Sameness
Hurrier/ Doormat	The Sorry Sinner/Lively Conformist	social malada-ptiveness versus social adaptiveness	nervous insecurity
Hurrier/Try Harder	The Angry Outsider/ Roving Adventurer	futility versus struggle	anger
Hurrier/Stiff Upper Lipper	The Fright-ened Loner/ Brave Individualist	emotion versus reason	fear and coldness
Doormat/Try Harder	The Humble Servant/ Contented Worker	niceness versus nastiness	lack of autonomy
Doormat/Stiff Upper Lipper	The Do-Gooder/ Generous Carer	compliance versus autonomy	"do-gooding"
Try Harder/ Stiff Upper Lipper	The Proud Loser/Quiet Achiever	crippled humiliation versus resil-ient strength	resentment

The rest of this chapter consists of elaborated accounts of each of the five basic personality types and brief descriptions of each of the ten compound types and each of the fifteen possible interpersonal relationships between the types.

For the sake of verbal simplicity, I will consistently stay with the pronoun "he" or "she" for each of the basic types and will arbitrarily denote one partner as "he" and the other as "she" in describing the interpersonal relationships. Of course, both men and women are equally able to have any of the types at the core of their personalities and in their relationships. However, sociologically, it can be observed that some types are more often expressed by men and some by women. In Britain, it seems that, stereotypically, women are more inclined than men to be the Doormat type and men more inclined than women to be the Stiff Upper Lipper type.

The Perfectionist

Basic nature

The Perfectionist expresses the religious view of life, which represents the accumulated wisdom of mankind about how we can live most happily in the face of our mortality. All religions offer us rewards for self-discipline and stoicism, accepted in the name of cosmic will and knowledge and meaning beyond our capacity to comprehend fully. The Perfectionist lives life religiously, whether or not she is an adherent of the orthodoxies of one of the named religions or only of her own idiosyncratic, self-created, self-imposed order and rigid discipline, by which she holds at bay her fear of death and gives meaning to her life. Without a basic minimum of the Perfectionist, we would each kill ourselves by accident in a very short time.

As a personality type, the Perfectionist is a close relative of the psychoanalytic obsessive-compulsive syndrome. It is associated with any too great or rigid structuring of everyday life in childhood. It is generally a safe hypothesis that anyone with a Roman Catholic or Jewish background, even if lapsed, or anybody brought up strictly in any other faith, has the Perfectionist central to her personality structure. The Perfectionist is exemplified in the scholastic pastime of arguing how many angels can dance on the point of a needle or the rabbinical one of whether or not it is lawful to eat an egg that was laid by a hen on the Sabbath. In Roman Catholics and others, the Perfectionist often focuses on sex, and that finds expression in behaviour which abstains from all sex unless associated with "perfect love", or else loves some people and has sex with others but never finds love and sex with one and the same person.

The Perfectionist is not especially prevalent in any socioeconomic class, but it is definitely most prevalent in countries where religion is a powerful part of the culture. It is much less common in Britain and other Protestant countries (because Roman Catholicism is much more Perfectionist than Protestanism).

The Perfectionist syndrome is usually temporarily dominant in the personalities of all latency-age children, at which stage of development children first become fully aware of the awfulness and horror of death. Children typically become very ritualistic about many things at this stage, secretly believing that they will die unless they think or do certain things in rigidly prescribed ways. Always or never stepping on the lines of the pavement is a commonplace manifestation of the Perfectionist syndrome in childhood. When it is effectively displaced in childhood, it finds outlets such as conscientiousness at school, collecting stamps and scout badges, and telling parents, with exactitude and excruciating detail, every single thing that happened at school today or in a horror film they have just seen. Incantations, curses, warding off the evil eye, and magic in general are all Perfectionist manifestations.

Overall, the Perfectionist is manifestly superstitious, critical, righteous, nit-picking, moralistic, meticulous, pedantic, sophistic, and joyless. "Right" or "wrong" is the usual first response to anybody or anything. Order versus disorder is a core dimension in the individual, and consistency is highly prized. Absolute certainty is sought, often at the very high price of creativity which depends on willingness to risk being mistaken. Because, as psychoanalysis has pointed out, the obsessive-compulsive personality needs an above-average intelligence quotient to contain its sophisticated verbal and ideational gymnastic, the Perfectionist is often dominant in very intelligent people. That is, being predominantly a Perfectionist can be taken to be a sufficient, although not necessary, indication of an above-average level of intelligence. Some of the most adaptive displacements and most constricting limitations of the Perfectionist are found in the stereotype of the academic.

Typical words used by the Perfectionist are: perfect/worthless, clean/dirty, should/shouldn't, obviously, as it were, believe, of course, depression, exactly, actually, precisely, It's not my fault, for my sins, to me personally. The Perfectionist's tone of voice is measured, accusatory, and didactic; facial expression is stern, severe, and flushed; posture is robot-like, rigid, stiff, and superior. Verbal and body attitudes include precision, over-qualification, meticulousness, fastidiousness, refusal to be interrupted, itemising and numbering of points while talking, pursing of bottom lip between forefinger and thumb, clearing throat, punctuating with finger and hand.

The Perfectionist is seeking to reaffirm a decision like, "I am not good enough" or "I am a worthless sinner".

Her deadly sin is Wrath, against God, and her core defensive aim is the reduction of anxiety by behaving in so blameless a way that Providence is not tempted. Introjected, the Perfectionist is self-righteously obedient to rules; projected, she gives exact and detailed instructions to others, uses big words, asks many questions, is nit-picking and fault-finding. Her favourite bad feelings are guilt and/or apprehensive worry. The Perfectionist generally refuses others' offers of help on the grounds that she would "rather do it myself and have it done properly", although, at least sometimes, she makes a total mess of things and/or interrupts others and gets in the way of their doing what they want to do. "I am worthless", accompanied by profound disappointment, is a typical payoff for this personality type, although it may also be projected as wrathful, judgemental shaming of others and, in extreme cases, murderous aggression.

The Perfectionist *saves and makes time and money*. She is hypochondriacal and is more than averagely inclined to die of heart disease. She is often chronically worried or depressed. Most extremely, the Perfectionist becomes psychotically depressed, when the rules she imposes on herself leave virtually no scope for any spontaneous behaviour at all, and the whole of her life becomes a frantic struggle to keep pace with "what has to be done".

The paradox of the Perfectionist syndrome is that, when it reaches a critical level, it changes from being the most wholesome, productive, and life-affirming attitude to life that there is, and becomes an insane living death through its hubristic attempt to be so in control—ultimately of God!—that death is averted forever. The Perfectionist's highest values are stability and certainty; but ultimate stability and certainty *is* death. The Perfectionist nature of us all is delineated with genius in Samuel Beckett's *Waiting for Godot*.

At her best, the Perfectionist is wise, purposeful, and has high moral standards; at her worst, she is depressed, full of rage, critical, autocratic, dogmatic, and bigoted. Her redemption resides in her gaining the permissions of tolerance, self-mockery, spontaneity, and general risk-taking.

Getting the best out of Perfectionists

Reassure them that there is nothing to worry about. When things go wrong, reassure them that it is not their fault. Be prompt in your responses to them, and arrive at appointments with them on time. Tease them playfully as, for example, one of my children, catching me anxiously trying to line up a bedspread exactly parallel to the edge of the bed, said, "Would you like me to get you a set-square?".

Never discount their worries. Instead, listen and let them know that you understand them; and do whatever you are willing and able to do to help them overcome their anxiety. Express your own, different values clearly and with conviction. Remind them that we all have to die, regardless of how carefully we live. Give them examples of how a certain degree of risk-taking is necessary for creative achievement. Suggest how other people hate their closed-minded dogmatism and bigotry, and that kindness is a greater virtue than rightness.

The Perfectionist, minus her intolerance, bigotry, and autocratic self-righteousness, is as wise, steadfast, warm, and good a person as you will ever know.

The Hurrier

Basic nature

The Hurrier syndrome is a defence against the fear of life. The Hurrier's premiss is that the universe is essentially malevolent and that life is to be endured painfully until relieved by death. The Hurrier deeply believes there is no meaning to life, and everything is futile. Nothing is satisfying, although he is willing to stay alive while he has energy to go on looking for the timeless and unconditional love of another human being that he believes would negate the pain of life. His quest for timeless and unconditional love is defeated over and over again, and suspicion and mistrust of other people is accumulated in these defeats. The Hurrier is overwhelmed by fear and consumed by hate. We all have some of the Hurrier syndrome in us, but how dominating it is in an individual's everyday life determines whether or not it is an appropriate descriptor of his manifest personality.

As a personality type, the Hurrier is a close relative of the paranoid syndrome. It is associated with the experience of abandonment in the first three years of life. The child's response includes the belief that his own intrinsic badness is the cause of his abandonment and that his parents, and the world, would be happier if he had not been born. Sexually, the Hurrier wants exclusively Child to nurturing Parent relationships with his partners. Sex is the price he is bound to pay for emotional security. Child to Child sex is frightening to him because to submit is to be violated. In the sex act itself, it is biologically the norm for the man to be the aggressor and for the woman to submit, so the sex life of a Hurrier woman is more obviously disturbed than the sex life of a Hurrier man.

Sociologically, the Hurrier is more often found in Britain in the working class and upper class, which perhaps elucidates the nature of the greater under-standing it is sometimes claimed the working and upper classes have with each other than either of them has with the middle class. In working-class families, children in whom the Hurrier personality is induced are typically latchkey kids who are obliged to come home from school to an empty house and to get their supper from a fast-food outlet; upper-class children in whom the Hurrier personality is induced are usually put in the care of paid nannies from birth and sent to boarding school at the earliest opportunity.

The Hurrier syndrome is a dominant theme at puberty, when being "anti" everything the child has previously been taught is now *de rigueur* to him. Containing the Hurrier impulse towards self-destructiveness is a core component of the stress of puberty experienced by both the child and his parents.

Overall, the Hurrier is manifestly chronically fear-ful and anxious, in a hurry, jittery, demanding, rest-less, shifty, manic, late, and generally unreliable and ungrateful. Core existential dimensions are mad-ness or murder, life and misery or death and peace, belonging or not belonging (which is often expressed as a childhood fantasy of having been adopted and really belonging to other, good parents), demand or withdraw, space and aloneness or claustrophobia and people. Hurriers are unable to be alone contentedly and yet, when they are with people, they give the impres-sion that they would rather be somewhere else or with somebody else. They are unable to sit still, they tap their fingers and feet impatiently, frown uncompre-hendingly at the person talking to them, often giving the impression to the other person that he or she has said something offensive. In truth, the Hurrier is on the run, all his life, from one or other parent, and is deeply convinced that his own intrinsic badness is responsible for the pain inflicted on him in childhood; and further, that if his parents ever actually catch up, they will murder him for his sins.

Typical words used by the Hurrier are "hurry up!", time, panic, anxiety, quickly, energy, tired, crazy, it's pointless, it's futile. The Hurrier says "I" but never "we". The Hurrier's tone of voice is agitated, demanding, staccato; facial expression is blank or frowningly non-comprehending, with brows knitted into vertical lines between the eyes. The Hurrier speaks rapidly and interrupts himself and others, is breathless and fidgety, impatient, drinks too much alcohol or takes drugs, and drives dangerously.

The Hurrier is seeking to reaffirm a decision like, "Life is meaningless and full of pain. The things I want will be given to me very briefly and then taken away forever, so it's best to reject people before they reject me." His deadly sin is Greed, and he is tyrannical in his needy demandingness. He asks for everything and ends up with nothing. Most sexual promiscuity is an expression of the Hurrier's quest. His favourite bad feelings are fear, panic, or terror, which is projected as "Let me be your baby". In contradistinction to his usual speed, there are times when he becomes totally immobile and may fall asleep in public.

He is an expert at "dumb insolence". "I am an outsider", "I am crazy", "Life is meaningless/futile/painful/ waiting for death", and "I suffer therefore I am" are typical final payoffs. Colin Wilson's *The Outsider* is a profound and elaborated description of the Hurrier.

The Hurrier *kills time and loses money*. He is prone to all kinds of addiction and to the necessity for surgical operations, and is more likely than average to die of drug abuse or other forms of self-inflicted bodily harm or neglect. Commonly, the Hurrier syndrome is manifest as chronic restless anxiety and fear. Most extremely, it is paranoid schizophrenia, in which the individual's thought processes are so disrupted that meaningful communication with others is broken and inadequate.

The paradox of the Hurrier syndrome is that, as well as being life-denying, it is also the adventurousness in us all, originally seen in the fearlessness of the infant who is totally ignorant of danger. To this extent, it is the antidote to the excesses of the Perfectionist in all of us which, unmitigated in its quest to avoid death, eventually achieves as-good-as-death psychological stultification, or even actual physical death. (I once heard of a Perfectionist housewife who every week found more and more items she "had to clean", until eventually she electrocuted herself cleaning the inside of a power point.)

At his best, the Hurrier is adventurous and sensitive and responsive to others' feelings; at his worst, he is hostile, greedy, passively resistant, and self-destructive. His redemption resides in his becoming willing to earn others' love and to love life for its own sake.

Getting the best out of Hurriers

Praise them for their efficiency. Enjoy their hectic spontaneity. Reassure them there is plenty of time.

Never be intimidated by their hysterical outbursts and demands. Instead, tell them quietly but firmly that you are leaving them for a short time but will be back soon and willing to listen when they are willing to talk calmly and rationally.

Be brave enough to be truly loving by setting firm limits to your willingness to indulge their greedy demands, for which you will eventually be rewarded with their achieved positive appreciation of life and contentment with what they have.

The Doormat

Basic nature

The Doormat is defending against the fear of responsibility. It is the response of the child to having won the Oedipal battle, that is, of having been more loved by his or her opposite-sexed parent than that parent loved his or her same-sexed parent. The consequence is the "spoiled brat" syndrome of the Doormat, which consists of a presumption of her entitlement to anything she wants from another. Along with this presumption goes a mixture of guilt and resentment towards the same-sexed parent, guilt for the illegitimacy of her victory over that parent, and resentment towards that parent for lacking the power legitimately to defeat the child. Doormat children also over-idealise their opposite-sexed parent, and pay the price of being unable appropriately to dissolve their sexual-emotional tie to that parent in order to find another whom they experience as being worthy of wholehearted love. The Doormat recapitulates this theme in all her relationships by manipulatively getting what she wants and denying responsibility for having "done" anything. The Doormat is nervously frightened of being "found out" and punished. When she is found out and confronted by another's wrath, she smiles abashedly. This smile represents both her triumph of revenge against her parents, who have so stunted her emotional growth, and a seductive bid to be forgiven on account of her child-like charm.

Control or be-controlled is the core dimension which the Doormat applies to all emotional transactions. Effectively, she says, "I will please you (controlled to controller), but when it's my turn, you have to please me (controller to controlled)". The dominant manifest feature of the Doormat syndrome is the individual's unwillingness, which she perceives as inability, to make any clear-cut or committed statement of her autonomous feelings, in case these feelings are morally wrong (which she was made to believe originally by her parents). The Doormat's aim is to get all that she wants by covert manipulation, and so deludes herself, as well as others, that things just "happen" to her, for which, of course, she can in no way be held responsible. Other people generally know they have been manipulated and are often very angry, but so slippery is the Doormat that it is usually very hard to prove the case against her, obvious as it actually is to the manipulated party.

As a personality type, the Doormat is a close relative of the psychoanalytic passive-aggressive syndrome. The Doormat presumes to read other people's minds, and considers having her own mind read to be a positive stroke. Because she doesn't know what she wants, she is glad to have other people tell her what she wants and give her whatever they decide is appropriate. When a response from her is demanded, she usually utters a platitude or cliché. Although she is thus denied autonomy or independence, the Doormat finds her compensation in being relieved of responsibility; if things go wrong, it is the other person's fault. The Doormat is so over-adapted that she is virtually cut off from her Free Child. She has been conditioned to believe that all feelings are made to order; she accepts, above all other considerations, her own obligation only to have *nice* feelings and to behave in accordance with propriety. She demands the same of others, and she is a busybody who doesn't mind her own business. She is unable to distinguish between Parent responsibility and Child feelings; for example, in looking after a crotchety old relative, the Doormat demands of herself that she always feel benevolent towards that relative as well as acting in accordance with Parent duty. She won't say "no" to any request, but often manages to forget that she ever said "yes". She secretly resents any demands made of her, and collects and stores resentment inside herself until, like a balloon, one more puff causes her to burst. The nearest innocent bystander may receive the full force of her explosive accusation that she is being treated like a doormat.

The Doormat syndrome can be presumed to be dominant in all only children. It is conditioned in families where respectability is emphasised and expression of Free Child wishes and feelings, especially bad feelings like jealousy, anger, vengeance, or hatred, are considered an embarrassment. Any authentic expression of feeling on the part of the child is likely to be responded to with, "That's not nice". Overall, these parents treat their children like accessories that improve their own appearance. But as long as the child responds obediently to such parents by only feeling and doing what she is told to feel and do, she is rewarded by having all her Adapted Child wishes granted before she is even aware of having them. Limitless love is granted so long as she remains a "good", irresponsible, dependent "baby".

The Doormat syndrome is overwhelmingly dominant in British society. My estimate is that about eighty per cent of the population exhibit it as their chief personality type. It typifies the English middle-class personality and is especially a feature of lower-middle-class respectability. "What will the neighbours think?" rules such families' lives.

Developmentally, the Doormat is most evident between the ages of about one and six years of age, during which stage the child is predominantly compliant, and uses coy manipulation to get what she wants.

Overall, the Doormat is manifestly manipulative, "nice" and "nasty", affected, pretentious, inauthentic, histrionic, nosey, "proper", socially devious, and querulous about the acceptability of her behaviour. "Am I good or naughty?" is a core issue. Safe pleasantness is sought rather than risky passion; blame and innocence, nurture or be nurtured, control or be controlled are her chief existential dimensions. Wriggling out of responsibility is her greatest triumph. Her free expression is stifled for the sake of emotional security, and yet she never feels fully assured that she is being "good enough" not to be abandoned.

Typical words used by the Doormat are: dear, really? nice, pleasant, y'know, kind of, sort of, I mean …, please yourself! embarrassed, super, you misunderstand me. She says "we" rather than "I" to avoid autonomy and responsibility. Her tone of voice is pleading, whining, dictating, questioning, and patronising. Her face is usually averted from looking directly at another person, her eyebrows are often permanently raised, resulting in deep horizontal lines on her forehead, her posture is humble and round-shouldered. Verbal and body attitudes include: nodding head repeatedly while another person is speaking, running fingers through or patting hair, checking appearance in a mirror.

The Doormat is seeking to reaffirm a decision like, "No matter what I do, others are never satisfied", or "Nobody gives me what I want". Her deadly sin is Falsehood. Her favourite bad feeling is embarrassment. Projectively, she tells people, resentfully, "That's not nice". She has angry outbursts that usually take others completely by surprise, and is often rude and inconsiderate of others, justified as being sick of being put upon. Introjectively, she withdraws sulkily. "Everybody misunderstands me", "Nobody ever gives me what I want", and "People treat me as if I am bad, but really I am good" are typical final payoffs, which may be vocalised as "Forget it!", meaning "Go to hell! You're the bad one, not me".

The Doormat *passes time and fritters money*. She is prone to indigestion—difficulty in stomaching the bad feelings she swallows—and psychosomatic ailments; she is more than averagely inclined to die of cancer. Commonly, the Doormat syndrome is expressed as an overwhelmingly conventional and banal personality. Most extremely, when her feelings are thoroughly repressed, she becomes the classical hysteric with conversion symptoms.

The paradox of the Doormat is that through her bid to please all of the people all of the time, she rarely pleases anybody, because she totally discounts people's individuality. Conformity is her most speciously valued virtue and, at best, she lives her life in the confines of a tiny gilded cage. Maintaining the sense of her own blamelessness is her desperate need, to which all other social aims are subsumed, and every transaction she has with another needs to culminate in her giving herself a merit stamp for good behaviour. She would be and do far more good if she were willing openly to acknowledge her guilt and resentment, which are hugely exaggerated by virtue of her compulsion to keep them hidden from herself and others.

At her best, the Doormat is pleasant, considerate of others' wishes, and generous; at her worst, she is passively aggressive, selfish, shallow, lacks consideration for others, and is self-righteously socially devious. Her redemption resides in her gaining the permissions to accept responsibility for the pains she causes others and to autonomously express her own feelings and desires.

Getting the best out of Doormats

Thank them politely for what they do for you. Stay near the surface of things in your communications with them. If you embarrass them with overly gutsy words or feelings, they will blush and not know how to respond and will resent you for it.

Never lose your own temper in response to their bad temper or rudeness. It is their covert aim to make you respond in a socially unacceptable way so they can slither out of awareness that they behaved badly, and they can then focus only on your bad behaviour. Instead, express your anger in a seething but controlled way. They may still refuse to accept responsibility for what they have done, by deciding they have been misunderstood, but they will be forced to awareness that something they did or said made you angry. If they have told you an outright lie, and you know that they know they have done so, don't fall into the trap of accusing them of it verbally; they will slither out of responsibility for it with the adroitness of Houdini. Instead, accuse them with a stony silence, while staring them straight in the eye; there is no escape from this.

If, out of your patient toughness, you eventually succeed in making a Doormat individual emotionally responsible and grown-up, you will have gained not only an authentic relationship with her but deep wisdom for your dealings with other people.

The Try Harder

Basic nature

The Try Harder is defending against the fear of failure. The Try Harder syndrome defines the world's losers, and the words "try" or "try hard" may very reliably be used to infer that whatever the person using it is setting out to do, he will fail. In a recent television programme about the Second World War, some film was shown of Neville Chamberlain returning from his second visit to Hitler, with his second bit of paper, and greeting the waiting crowds by saying, "When I was a little boy, I always used to say, 'If at first you don't succeed, try, try again'"!

The Try Harder personality is the response of the child to having lost the Oedipal battle in a wrong way, namely by the excessive aggression of his same-sexed parent. The consequence in the child is fearful timidity towards the same-sexed parent and an absence of self-esteem. The love of the opposite-sexed parent may be assured, but the child experiences the same-sexed parent as a powerful barrier preventing him gaining intimate access to his opposite-sexed parent. The child is humiliated and full of rage towards the same-sexed parent, and is ambivalent about whether or not to dare to fight the same-sexed parent for the right to intimacy with the opposite-sexed parent. He believes that if he fought, he could be defeated and even more humiliated than he is already in his passive acceptance of inferiority; if victorious, he would feel himself to be the murderer of his same-sexed parent. So the Try Harder hovers between the contrary impulses of impotent passivity and raging pugnacity, which he resolves by *trying* to gain his share of success. This "trying" is carefully calculated by his Adapted Child to achieve neither of the fearful outcomes of accepting his essential inferiority or of murdering his same-sexed parent. He uses up an enormous amount of energy, as if frantically treading water in order not to drown, but also getting nowhere. Procrastination is a favourite device, and the Try Harder recapitulates this theme in all that involves his self-esteem, particularly in relationship to worldly success, but also in intimate relationships. His pose may be humble or arrogant, or alternating, but whichever side of the coin is his chosen mask, the other side will be very evident to any sensitive observer. His own and others' aggression cause him a lot of trouble.

As a personality type, impotent envy or admiration, and arrogant pugnacity or self-deprecating humility are the core dimensions of the Try Harder. It is important to distinguish between envy and jealousy. Envy is purely destructive and is based on two false premises: that if I had what another has I would surely be happy; and that other person, having what I believe would make me happy, must be happier than I am. Jealousy, when exaggerated, is also an expression of destructive, low self-esteem, but when it is unexaggerated, it is a natural and healthy expression of the wish to be loved by a loved other, mixed with a hatred of a rival for that love. Jealousy is a mixture of love and hate; envy is pure hate.

The Try Harder is always putting all his eggs in one grandiose basket, forever being about to make the big time in whatever realm his essential need to fail is focused. In his head, he is forever competitive and forever comparing himself to others as superior or inferior to them in some way or other. The typical final payoff of, "I'm not as good as I think I am" is a close relative of Alfred Adler's inferiority complex, whose compensation is found in both being "about to make it" and of copping out of all competition with a rationalisation such as, "I could be the greatest if I could be bothered". In reality, the Try Harder is neither as great nor as incapable of achievement as he experiences himself to be. The Try Harder buys a ticket in a lottery and excitedly thinks of nothing else but winning until the lottery is drawn; or is out of work and expects that something will turn up; or blames his tools when he does a botched job; or doesn't attempt the job at all on the grounds that it is "impossible". He is a great believer in luck; others get the good sort, while he gets the bad. (In fact, luck—good or bad—hardly exists, except in such matters as just catching or just missing a bus, which can be seen to cancel out to zero after a very few occurrences.)

The Try Harder is made in families in which one or both parents are resentful or bitter about their lot and blame other people or society for the fact that they have not got what they wanted in life. Their children are not allowed to be pleased with themselves; if they dare to achieve things and be proud of the fact, they are quickly put down with, "Who do you think you are?" The Try Harder personality is a response to a very powerful message received against competing with Mother or Father. It is sex-linked, that is, a Try Harder woman is unwilling to compete with her mother, and a Try Harder man is unwilling to compete with his father. The Child ego state of the child is terrified of losing Mother's or Father's love by making them envious if they dare to achieve something their parents wanted to but never did. Often, the Parent messages given are vociferously, "We want you to do/have all the things we never had the opportunity to do/have". The Depression, the Second World War, and early motherhood are often invoked by recent generations of parents as the external circumstances that account for their failures in life; the children believe them and are thus made loath to take what they see as unfair advantages that the world is offering them compared with what it offered their parents. True, there are external social circumstances that stand in the way of people getting all they want when they want it, but external circumstances are never the whole truth. A spirit of aliveness and joy can be found in the direst external circumstances, as can misery and bitterness be found amongst the materially most privileged. Obstacles empower winners and defeat losers; winners see the doughnut, losers see the hole.

Sociologically, in Britain the Try Harder personality is eminently working-class Conservative to the point of "facism" or may be militantly trade-unionist. "Knowing one's place" rules such families' lives.

Developmentally, the Try Harder is very much in evidence in adolescence, when aggressive hostility towards the same-sexed parent is expressed by the child as he struggles to achieve his confidence as a competent adult. The demands on the child to work hard to pass examinations exploit, in a positive way, the natural aggressive-competitive impulses of this stage of development.

Overall, the Try Harder is competitive, angry, aggressive, pathetic, humble, helpless, grandiose, conceited, bitter, militant, and sarcastically discounting of others. Above all, he is envious of others. The Try Harder starts a dozen projects and finishes none of them. He seeks out the company of people he can look down on, although he is also eager to be a hanger-on of some other people he can look up to. What he cannot cope with is the essential reality that we are all better than most people at a few things, not as good as most people at a few things, and equal with every other human being in nearly every respect. For him, it is competing on the centre court at Wimbledon or not playing tennis at all, winning the Nobel Prize or discounting all his achievements. He wants all or nothing and so gets nothing.

Typical words used by the Try Harder are: Can you …? could/couldn't, impossible, superior/inferior, fail/succeed, I don't know, it's hard, lucky/unlucky, I'm better than/not as good as you/him/her. His tone of voice is angry and sarcastic; facial expression is puzzled, irritated, and worried. Verbal and body attitudes include sitting forward, elbows on knees, chin in hand, asking more than one question at a time, not answering the question asked, stuttering, having an impatient manner and clenched fist.

The Try Harder is seeking to reaffirm a decision like, "I'm a failure" or "I'm not as good as I think I am". His deadly sins are Envy and Sloth. His core defensive aim is to leave open to doubt whether he is a success or failure. Success would mean symbolically murdering his envious, same-sexed parent; failure would be wholeheartedly to admit that that parent was right. Projectively, he tells others, "That's good enough", or "Well, it's better than nothing"; introjectively, he says, "I could do that if I wanted to", or "It's not worth it". The typical final payoff of "I'm a failure" is projected as "Well, you were overstepping yourself, weren't you?".

The Try Harder personality *wastes time and money*. He is prone to headaches and all stress-related illnesses, such as ulcers. He is more than averagely inclined to die as a consequence of accidents. Commonly, this personality is manifest as conceit or envy and bitterness. Most extremely, it becomes pathological narcissism and/or schizoid grandiosity.

The paradox of the Try Harder personality is that its defence against its fear of failure makes the success it longs for impossible, because all success involves failure along the way. It avoids both hell and heaven; it lives in purgatory. Only when the Try Harder stops making excuses for his parents' failures and bitterness will he, by appropriate persistent effort, achieve his own healthy self-esteem and be able to take pleasure in others' self-esteem, without envy or admiration, but as equal to equal.

At his best, the Try Harder is passionately committed to his causes, is persistent, and has sympathy for the underdog; at his worst, he is pugnacious, arrogant, aggressive, and blaming of circumstances for his own failures. His redemption resides in his gaining permissions to "do better than" his same-sexed parent and to allow himself to both fail and, in due course, to succeed.

Getting the best out of Try Harders

Ignore the competitiveness implicit in the remarks they make. For example, to "Have you only got a 17-inch television? Mine's 26-inch", respond, "That sounds nice", implying, "I'm glad you've got what you want. I've got what I want, too. I don't envy you or expect you to envy me." Or, in response to their obsessive concern with being superior by virtue of having the right answer, such as, "I knew it was going to rain today. You said it wouldn't. I was right", reply blandly,

"Yes, you were". (Try Harders are so frightened of their experience of humiliation if they turn out to be wrong in factual matters that they often do not make open predictions at all, but only after the event say, "I knew it would rain ages before you said it would").

Never let them off what they have committed themselves to do; doing so implies that you have as low expectations of them as they have of themselves. Instead, express anger towards them for not getting on with whatever it is; this powerfully implies that you have no doubt about their capability. They will complain that you are tyrannical and heartless, but your willingness to do this thankless task will be the mark of your love, which will eventually be rewarded with their transformation into healthily self-confident and potent companions.

The Stiff Upper Lipper

Basic nature

The Stiff Upper Lipper syndrome is the defence against the fear of rejection. It is the Oedipal response of the child to feeling redundant to the self-sufficient, closed, symbiotic relationship between his parents, irrespective of whether the relationship between the parents is essentially happy or essentially unhappy. The consequence is that the child neither identifies with his same-sexed parent, nor feels appreciated by his opposite-sexed parent. Consequently, Stiff Upper Lip children believe they lack the characteristics that are needed to be loveworthy, and they respond with lonely self-sufficiency. The Stiff Upper Lipper recapitulates this theme in all his subsequent relationships by a mask of aloofness and invulnerability to others, which prevents others making intimate contact with him; thus he avoids being rejected at the price of avoiding intimacy. "I don't need or want anybody" is the lie he tells himself and others.

As a personality type, self-sufficiency or rejection is the core dimension which the Stiff Upper Lipper applies to all relationships between people. He longs for closeness, but believes he is intrinsically unloveworthy and, therefore, has to do without intimacy altogether, or be satisfied with a relationship with a very needy other whose neediness alone will bind that other to him.

The Stiff Upper Lipper makes a virtue out of what he sees as a necessity to be solely dependent on himself for strokes to his Child. Convinced that his Child is essentially unloveworthy, he never asks for any strokes from others for his Child, and puts his Child last when choosing, on any occasion, which ego state is the appropriate one to be in. Because, biologically, it is natural for the man to "ask" the woman for intimacy and for the woman to respond to this asking, the sex life of a Stiff Upper Lip man is more obviously curtailed than is the sex life of a Stiff Upper Lip woman. Even when the Stiff Upper Lipper cannot avoid noticing that another is stroking his Child, he disbelieves the authenticity of the strokes being offered, and either huffily dismisses the other person on the presumption that she is a crawler or else politely accepts the stroke without allowing it to nourish him. He is only able to accept a few strokes for his responsible Parent and sensible Adult.

The Stiff Upper Lipper is induced in families in which children are expected to be seen and not heard. Expressing emotion, particularly painful emotion, is frowned on as bad form, and kissing and cuddling are positively discouraged. The Stiff Upper Lipper is also induced in families in which there are no Parent messages to support it, but it is simply a response to circumstantial unlovingness towards and general emotional neglect of the child. Typically, one or other of the parents is narcissistically embroiled in his or her own Child's needs and the other parent is so busy coping with the narcissistic parent's demands that neither parent has energy left over for giving to the Child of the child. The child assumes the Rescuer role towards his needy parent's Victim, by which means he makes continual but doomed-to-fail attempts to "make Mummy or Daddy better". The Victim parent often explicitly invites the child to "Parent" him or her but inevitably turns Persecutor, so the child ends up the true victim of the parent's exploitation. Stiff Upper Lip children are never allowed to be real children—carefree, playful, demanding, and indulged—only little adults, worldly-wise, sad, and constantly burdened by their awareness of others' suffering.

Like all other types, the Stiff Upper Lipper personality may predominate in any individual in any culture, but sociologically, the Stiff Upper Lipper is a very English middle-class and upper-class syndrome, and the British public school ethos systematically indoctrinates it. Traditionally, children at public and other boarding schools typically have had the Stiff Upper Lipper imposed on them by teachers and caretakers as a moral imperative, with the aim of producing stiff-upper-lipped ladies and gentlemen, ready to serve the community with impermeable emotional invulnerability. Stoicism is the chief Parent currency supporting the Stiff Upper Lipper.

Developmentally, the Stiff Upper Lipper is most evident during latency, when the Adult ego state predominates in the personality, and all children are less emotionally involved with others than they were in their earlier years or will be again from the onset of puberty.

Overall, the Stiff Upper Lipper is manifestly cold, aloof, self-contained, uninvolved, invulnerable, unemotional, independent, and a loner. He talks about feelings, but never shows them. "Strength" versus "weakness" is a core dimension; self-discipline is displayed and respected in others, while mawkishness or any form of wearing one's heart on one's sleeve is deplored. Duty *is* pleasure. People who express their emotions are judged boring. The Stiff Upper Lipper longs most of all to be given the love that he, in fact, rejects if gratuitously offered him, because he cannot believe in it. He asks for nothing, and so gets nothing.

It was the Stiff Upper Lipper in Captain Oates that "went out for a while" to die on Scott's last voyage. It is the Stiff Upper Lipper who is the last to leave a sinking ship, is marvellous in a crisis, gets on with things, goes for brisk walks, and gets up at 6 a.m. every day of the year to go for a swim. He never cries or whines or complains, and a Stiff Upper Lipper man may wear a moustache to keep his upper lip hidden just in case, despite his best efforts, it should slacken. The Stiff Upper Lipper is deeply lonely and stroke-deprived but is usually seen by others only as aloof and stand-offish.

Typical words used by the Stiff Upper Lipper are: strong/weak, boring, pull yourself together, I don't care, no comment, vulnerable, duty, childish, it's no good getting upset/crying over spilt milk, you don't appreciate what I'm saying, I feel that …, that makes me feel. The Stiff Upper Lipper says "you" or, even more stiffly, "one" instead of "I". His tone of voice is monotonic and dispassionate; his face is moulded, cold, hard, expressionless; posture is erect, rigid, and frozen. Verbal and body attitudes include an over-straight back, legs crossed, apparently being totally in Adult but actually in Adapted Child, pulling socks up, excessive expression of appreciation for anything received.

The Stiff Upper Lipper is seeking to a reaffirm a decision like, "I am unappreciated" or "I am unloveworthy". His deadly sin is Pride. Projectively, he is a Rescuer, who offers unwanted help to others, but also accuses others of being too demanding, finds them boring, and expresses invulnerability towards them. Introjectively, he never complains, whatever the circumstances, and waits passively and inflexibly for others to make the first approach. His favourite bad feeling is being unappreciated, and his final payoff is, "I am unlovable".

The Stiff Upper Lipper *uses time and money*. He keeps himself healthy to avoid "weakness" and the vulnerability of being ill; but the Stiff Upper Lipper is also often found amongst people who commit suicide without warning, taking others completely by surprise. He is also more than averagely inclined to die of a stroke. (Note the canny connection to "stroke" deprivation.) The Stiff Upper Lipper personality is expressed as resigned loneliness. Most extremely, it becomes autism, in which there is a total non-reactivity to other people, that is, no strokes whatsoever from other people are acknowledged.

The paradox of the Stiff Upper Lipper is that his defence against the fear of rejection makes the intimacy he longs for impossible, because the achievement of intimacy involves being open to others, which includes the risk of rejection. His adherence to the myth that the avoidance of the pleasures of intimacy is a fair enough price to pay for the avoidance of pain is tantamount to emotional death. Only when he drops his pride and his selfishness in only giving and never allowing others the pleasure of giving to him, can he receive the love he longs for and intrinsically deserves as much as anybody else.

At his best, the Stiff Upper Lipper is reliable, self-sufficient, and considerate of others' needs; at his worst, his is cold, aloof, invulnerable to others, and profoundly lonely. His redemption consists of his gaining permission to ask for and accept love from others, willingly experiencing rejection along the way.

Getting the best out of Stiff Upper Lippers

Praise them for their consideration and kindness. Praise them for their reliability. When they invite you to dinner or for a treat that will cost them money or effort, tell them that you would like, for a change, to treat them instead. Hold back from effusiveness toward them and respect their occasional need for privacy and aloneness. Give them strokes through irony. For example, "I must say, you're the most unreliable person I know", which they can accept, with a smile, more easily than a straightforward positive stroke. Be warmly appreciative of any presents they give you.

Never try to force them to directly express their sad or lonely feelings; they will only deny them and retreat from any intimacy you have so far achieved. Never shout or express your own emotions hysterically in their presence. If you do, they will crumble inwardly, and silently remove themselves from your presence, wearing a stony mask, and you will have achieved nothing. Nevertheless, they need to be told calmly and clearly that feelings, not reason, make the world go round, and there are times when being "uninvolved" is not the proud virtue they claim but cruel inhumanity.

More than anything else, Stiff Upper Lippers long to be convinced that *you feel loved by them* and are glad of it. Once they are so convinced, they will shed their brittle armour for you alone, and be yours forever.

Ten compound personality types

The five basic personality types make up the substance of everybody's Adapted Childs; and the Adapted Child is involved in nearly everything we think, feel, and do in the course of our lives. But these elements are mixed and matched in a large variety of ways in individual human beings. Some people have one element dominatingly and overwhelmingly present in most of their everyday transactions, while others seem to make use, in quick succession, of all five elements. However, generally speaking, most people seem to concentrate on two basic types to confirm their core painful existential position, whose reaffirmation is a chief motivator— however unconscious—of all that we think, feel, and do throughout our lives.

Thus, the ten possible pairings of the five basic types describe ten common personality sub-types. Usually the elements seem to combine in an additive way; sometimes one of the pair, notably the other element in most combinations with the Hurrier, is an attempt to nullify the meaning of the principal element at the core of the personality. However, at the deepest level, each pair represents both a conflict and the resolution of that conflict in the individual. (See table, p. 72)

While the isotopic manifestations in thought, feeling, and behaviour of the singular personality types are multifarious, their essentially elementary nature makes a fairly comprehensive account of each of them possible. The compounds, on the other hand, are manifestations of the enormous overall complexity of any personality, so any compound description is bound to be a caricature of any particular human being it describes.

Below are very brief archetypal descriptions of the ten compound personality types, their core existential dichotomies, and the redemptive, transformative tasks that turn the hang-ups associated with them into achieved talents.

Perfectionist–Hurrier

This is the Uncommitted Doubter. Potentially, because it holds in balance the most atavistic and archetypal impulses in us all, the fear of death and the quest for excitement, it represents the ideal of psychological health, but it also contains within it the seeds of some of the best-known and intractable dis-eases that are familiar to psychotherapists, including alcoholism, bi-polar disorder, and anorexia nervosa. Whether the net result of the internal balancing act of the personality is equanimity and healthy, sceptical open-mindedness, or an excruciating and overwhelming combined terror of and wish for insanity or death or something in between, depends on how intensely the two elements are experienced in the individual. From my experience, the difference between essential health and essential pathology in this compound is reflected in whether or not the individual has found a meaning in life which transcends the mundane goals of everyday living, and can be expressed through purposeful endeavour. For many people, parenthood is the prototype of all such endeavours, but anything that the individual decides is, in the long run, profoundly worth doing serves the same need. If such a purpose is not found, the individual forces himself to consume all the energy of his dilemma in the dilemma itself, in an escalating spiral of the Perfectionist catching up with the Hurrier and over-stepping the mark, which necessitates an extra spurt of the Hurrier to catch up with the Perfectionist, which oversteps the mark … to the limiting equilibrium, in its most pathological form, of manic-depressive psychosis or death by suicide or accident. Like right-wing and left-wing political parties, the Perfectionist and the Hurrier are manifestly opposites and capable of holding each other in check, yet they meet in an implosive fusion of fascism/communism when each becomes extreme.

The core existential dichotomy of this compound is security or danger, which justifies the expression of excessive caution and bravado. The compound decision being served is something like, "I and the whole world are either mad or bad, but I'm not sure which". When the Uncommitted Doubter transforms guilt into organisation and panic into efficiency, he may become the truly Passionate Philosopher.

Perfectionist–Doormat

This is the Righteous Blamer. Perfectionist morality is powerfully brought to bear as a justification for the conventional goodness that defends the Doormat's emotional insecurity. Child feelings and Parent beliefs are heavily contaminated. The core existential dichotomy of this compound is control or be controlled, which justifies the expression of intense emotionality in response to everybody and everything. Righteous Blamers are typically very successful "organisation" people, eminently capable as they are both of controlling and being controlled, and they are often workaholics.

The compound decision being served is something like, "If I make the wrong decision, I will be culpable and feel guilty, but so long as I make no choice, I am being good, so nobody can blame me for what goes wrong." When the Righteous Blamer transforms guilt into organisation and feeling misunderstood into flexibility, he may become the truly Responsible Leader.

Perfectionist–Try Harder

This is the Fighter of Lost Causes. The Perfection-ist component is an obsessive *idée fixe* about what should be done to set the world to rights, but the Try Harder component makes sure that the goal is unre-alistic. This personality is aggressively single-minded and dismissive of all topics of conversation but its own hobby horse. A core existential belief of this personality is that Adult reason and Parent belief are one and the same thing. "Moral and stupid" is opposed to "rebel-lious and clever"; super-reasonableness flatly rejects as irrelevant any Child feelings which may question the absolute rightness of the cause.

Power and pride or submission and humiliation is the core dichotomy of this compound, which justifies the expression of blame and envy. The compound decision being served is something like, "Nobody lives up to my ideals and I'm not as good as I should be either. If I do bad things, other people may let me off, and then I am relieved, but I would feel more loved if they punished me and told me what I've done wrong." When the Fighter of Lost Causes transforms guilt into organ-isation and fear of failure into persistence, she may become the truly Committed Champion.

Perfectionist–Stiff Upper Lipper

This is the Cold Intellectual. The two elements in this compound are the only two elements that do not, in some way, imply inhibition of thought. This compound throws interesting light on British, as contrasted with European, and particularly French, thought. Since the rationality of the Perfectionist is an essential ingredi-ent of all intellectuality, and the Perfectionist is much more predominant a cultural element of Continental Europe than Britain, Britain is a comparatively non-intellectual country. But when, in Britain, an individual Perfectionist thinker produces an idea, it is likely to have the special British advantage of Stiff Upper Lip empiricism as well as Perfectionist rationality. Histori-cally, it is probably a fair claim that, as a nation, we don't think much but, when we do, our Stiff Upper Lip pragmatism gives our ideas an ultimate advantage over the purely rational ideas of our singularly Perfectionist French rivals.

Being rejected or self-denial is the core existen-tial dichotomy of this compound, which justifies the expression of superior aloofness. The compound deci-sion being served is something like, "Other people can-not cope with my needs as well as their own. Since their needs are greater than mine, I have no right to ask for anything from them. So long as I need nothing from others, I will not be tempted to ask for anything, and so I can remain blameless." When the Cold Intel-lectual transforms guilt into organisation and feeling unappreciated into being resilient, he may become the truly Independent Thinker.

Hurrier–Doormat

This is the Sorry Sinner. The Hurrier is usually at the core of this compound, with the Doormat taken on board in a desperate bid to find the rules of interper-sonal behaviour that will release the individual from her pain and isolation. Sorry Sinners are usually popu-lar for being lively amongst the people they work with, but they are inclined to have episodic outbursts of rudeness and bad temper that may threaten their job security.

The core existential dichotomy of this compound is terrifying aloneness or suffocating reassurance, which justifies the expression of clinging dependency and paranoid rejection. The compound decision being served is something like, "I could love life if only I could find somebody to love me in the way I want to be loved, that is, with unconditional love from the other's Parent to my Child. I try so hard to be good, and sometimes I think I am loved, but then the other person always soon stops loving me and tells me to go to hell." When the Sorry Sinner transforms panic into efficiency and feeling misunderstood into flexibility, she may become the truly Lively Conformist.

Hurrier–Try Harder

This is the Angry Outsider. It is Hell's Angels, bully boys, and criminals. Less extremely, it is con men, militant trade unionists, or militant women's movement … or militant anything. The passive version is the laid-back drop-out. In general, this personality is snarling, derisive, and cynical. Often, it is utterly joyless, but sometimes the underlying Free Child quest for joy finds expression in a hare-versus-tortoise-like attitude to life, in which the individual is always moving from one short-lived enthusiasm to the next.

The core existential dichotomy of this compound is rage or futility, which justifies the expression of pugnacious sarcasm. The compound decision being served is something like, "There's nothing you can do for me or give me and I'll sock you one if you try. I'm no good but neither are you. The world is one big shit heap." When the Angry Outsider transforms panic into efficiency and fear of failure into persistence, she may become the truly Roving Adventurer.

Hurrier–Stiff Upper Lipper

This is the Frightened Loner. Any individual in whose personality this compound is a central feature has been unequivocally stroke-deprived in childhood to a criminal extent. These are the battered babies, the children in care, and, horrifically—in my direct experience—many of the most materially privileged children in Britain, the sons and daughters of the upper class. So lonely are these people and so painful and futile does life seem inescapably to be to them, that they are compelled continuously to do battle with self-destructive impulses that goad them to find, in death, the only possible release from their torment. Brave adventurers and heroes, such as solo yachtsmen, are probably the people best adapted to this compound in themselves.

The core existential dichotomy of this compound is reject or be rejected, which justifies the expression of futility and boredom. The compound decision being served is something like, "I can make no sense of people or the world. The world is strange and cold and I am lost in it. Anyone who loves me is a shit." When the Frightened Loner transforms panic into efficiency and feeling unappreciated into resilience, he may become the truly Brave Individualist.

Doormat–Try Harder

This is the Humble Servant. This personality is stereotypically working-class and lower-middle-class respectability. It is timid, proper, utterly conventional, knows its place, and does not question life as it finds it. But it is not without pride. Knowing its own place implies the obligation for others to know their place too, exemplified in the lady's maid who defines herself as above her background by virtue of the status of her employer but, equally important, below her employer.

The core existential dichotomy of this compound is niceness or success. The compound decision being served is something like "As long as people do as they are told, no harm will come to them." When the Humble Servant transforms feeling misunderstood into flexibility and fear of failure into persistence, she may become the truly Contented Worker.

Doormat–Stiff Upper Lipper

This is the Do-Gooder. While it may predominate in an individual of any nationality, this personality is the stereotypical personality of the English: courteous, considerate, nice but sometimes nasty, practical and helpful, but also aloof and uptight, and secretly resentful of the impositions of others on their goodwill.

The core dichotomy of this compound is control or vulnerability, which justifies the expression of resentful withdrawal. The compound decision being served is something like, "I look after others when, by rights, they should be looking after me." When the Do-Gooder transforms feeling misunderstood into flexibility and feeling unappreciated into resilience, she may become the truly Generous Carer.

Try Harder–Stiff Upper Lipper

This is the Proud Loser. Proud Losers do not make a fuss about their loneliness and despair; rather they timidly Try Hard to make their feelings and wishes known and to fulfil their ambitions. But they so under-express themselves as to ensure that their cries and ideas remain unheard and unvalued. They typically dislike but endure their work, whatever it is. They are not much noticed in their jobs, and they tend to withdraw into their private dreams.

The existential dichotomy of this compound is frustration or resignation, which justifies the expression of envious aloofness. The compound decision being served is something like, "The struggle to get what I want is not worthwhile because successful people never appreciate my worth, so I'd rather be with losers who I know are inferior to me." When the Proud Loser transforms fear of failure into persistence and feeling unappreciated into resilience, he may become the truly Quiet Achiever.

Fifteen types of relationships

In our intimate relationships, the discriminations we make between people with our Free Child, Adult, and Parent are fairly crude. Like other animals, our Free Child's essential narcissism usually dictates that we prefer others who reflect back to us our own image, mostly in terms of colouring, shape, and size. Subsidiarily, our Parent prefers people of similar background and education to ourselves. Our Adult has little, if any, say. But the turn-ons that excite us most are all informed by our Adapted Child. Simple, physical orgasm is not a patch on "the real thing", which is, uniquely for human beings, a physical response compounded with emotionality, and consists of a huge variety of possibilities that Freud subsumed in the dichotomy of sadism and masochism. There are pleasures in our pains and pains in our pleasures, and the compulsive nature of our Adapted Child testifies to this truth. It feels and expresses our passionate involvement with the world and other people.

There are fifteen possible relationships between the Adapted Child of one person and the Adapted Child of another: five relationships between like types and ten relationships between different types. Since most people have two types at the core of their personalities, the Adapted Child to Adapted Child relationship of any two people is typically made up of four discrete ways of relating, each of which has its own pleasures and pains. Given that there is no escaping the predominance of our Adapted Childs in our relationships, it can be very useful to a couple to analyse the Adapted Child to Adapted Child part of their relationship into its separate components. By this means, the couple are able self-consciously to choose to act out the pleasanter aspects of their relationship and avoid the nastier aspects, while still realistically acknowledging the inevitable centrality of Adapted Child to Adapted Child transactions in their total relationship.

Out of many years' experience, my diagnoses of the fifteen possible couplings between the five personality types can be taken as very reliable, although the descriptions are inevitably exaggerated stereotypes when applied to the reality of a particular relationship. It is merely my intention to communicate the general flavour of what to expect from each of the pairings; the usefulness of my descriptions will depend on the reader's willingness to translate my comments imaginatively into the realm of his or her own experience. Nevertheless, I hope that my comments reflect sufficiently commonplace experience that the reader will, in many cases, readily match his or her own observations to mine. A summary table of the advantages and disadvantages of each of the fifteen pairings is given at the end of this chapter. (Remember that when I designate one of a pair as "he" and the other as "she",

I do so for the sake of verbal simplicity. Men and women are instrinsically equally able to adopt either role in all the possible pairings; and the pairings can equally apply to relationships between two people of the same sex).

Perfectionist and Perfectionist

Like most couplings of like-to-like, this pair usually get on well with each other. They are apt to be united by their common beliefs, and so long as they do not disagree fundamentally about what is and is not important in life, they give each other the security of feeling right about things. Their life together tends to be ritualistic, extremely well organised and ordered. However, if they do disagree fundamentally about their values in life, they will bicker and criticise each other interminably and probably end up feeling intransigent mutual hatred. A negative Perfectionist–Perfectionist relationship is epitomised in the internecine war in Northern Ireland, the Israel–Arab conflict, and in all the religious wars that have ever been fought.

Perfectionist and Hurrier

At the profoundest levels of their personalities, the individuals who form this couple are supremely well matched. When referred to the deepest psychological level, the Perfectionist and the Hurrier are expressions of the fear of death and the temptation of death respectively. To this extent, the Perfectionist is a cowardly stick-in-the-mud and the Hurrier a brazen daredevil. They are able to cancel out the unhealthy extreme that each on its own stands for and to create instead an optimally healthy balance in their relationship between organisation and efficiency, thrift and extravagance, caution and daring, structure and spontaneity … and many other adaptive compromises between a wide range of polarities in life. Transactionally, the Perfectionist tends to play the role of the sometimes indulgent and sometimes controlling Parent to the sometimes charming and sometimes exasperating Child of the Hurrier. The only possibility of serious harm in this relationship arises when one or both express their Adapted Child at a very high pitch. When this occurs, the Adapted Childs may escalate each other in a vicious spiral until they lose their separate identities and collide in murderous/suicidal insanity.

Perfectionist and Doormat

This is often a very stable and contented relationship based on agreed dominance and submission roles. The Perfectionist is the boss and the Doormat is happily obedient. The Perfectionist's quest for having things be and be done exactly the way he wants is fulfilled and, complementarily, the Doormat is profoundly reassured in knowing she is doing the right and good thing. "You have done well", given by the Perfectionist, is usually happily received by the Doormat as a positive stroke, even though others might resent the patronage implied. However, because of their contented equilibrium, the Perfectionist tends to lack the stimulating challenge to his rigidity of outlook, and the Doormat gains no permission to live outside the bounds of her repressive conventionality. Such couples sometimes find expression of the suppressed side of the Adapted Child in each of them through episodes in which the Doormat expresses some fleeting defiant rebelliousness and the Perfectionist responds with angry criticism. But the Perfectionist quickly controls the outburst of the Doormat and things usually return rapidly to their normal peace and calm.

Perfectionist and Try Harder

This is often an obviously unhappy relationship based on open warfare. They are very critical of each other; but the Perfectionist, who tends to be the more intelligent in this partnership, is usually the one who, in arguments, consistently ends up being the victorious Persecutor while the Try Harder ends up being the humiliated Victim. The Perfectionist is using the Try Harder to project her own feeling of worthlessness out of herself, while the Try Harder is continually reinforced in his fundamental belief that "No matter how hard I try, I'll never be successful enough". The Perfectionist often threatens to leave the Try Harder, but she knows secretly that she is dependent on the Try Harder for her needed feeling of superiority. Both know their relationship is likely to continue in its often violent unhappiness for a long time.

Perfectionist and Stiff Upper Lipper

This couple is usually united by a puritanical attitude to life. Often, they are both ambitious and work very hard to achieve their goals. The Perfectionist easily accommodates to the Stiff Upper Lipper's view that "reliability is the better part of love"; and the Stiff Upper Lipper pleases the Perfectionist by being willing to get on with things without complaining. They are likely to enjoy conversations with each other that are serious, playfully critical, and sophisticatedly ironical. They are unlikely to cause each other pain, but they tend to reinforce rather than positively modify each other's essential over-dutifulness at the expense of Free Child spontaneity and pleasure.

Hurrier and Hurrier

Since the deep intention of the Hurrier in relation to others is "I'll reject you before you reject me", a relationship between two people who are principally Hurriers is so unstable that it is unlikely to be formed at all. However, in contradiction of the deep but usually denied aim of not maintaining intimacy, the Hurrier is phenomenally obsessed with finding lasting love. So when two Hurriers meet, they are likely to experience themselves as falling overwhelmingly in love at first sight; and they often fall straight into bed with each other at their first meeting. The relationship ends with a bang rather than a whimper, a short time later, when one of them simply doesn't turn up to an arranged meeting, or in some way expresses as much hateful lack of regard for the other as he or she expressed loving commitment at their first meeting. When Hurrier to Hurrier is a minor component of a couple's relationship, it will probably find expression in either or both of them slamming out of the house without saying where they are going or for how long. Sometimes they get drunk or "stoned out of their minds" in each other's company, but the isolation each of them then feels is as great as it would be if they were each alone.

Hurrier and Doormat

From the point of view of the Hurrier, this relationship can be nearly as good for him as a relationship with a Perfectionist. Although the Perfectionist is more capable than the Doormat of providing the Hurrier with the profound existential control he so desperately needs, the Doormat can offer the Hurrier a great deal of reassurance. It is as if the Hurrier is saying, "It's no good expecting love to last. People give it to you for a little while, but then they inevitably withdraw it and you are left alone." To which the Doormat replies, "I know exactly how you feel, how frightening it is to think of being left alone. But you know it's not inevitable. So long as you are good, the people who love you will stay with you forever. Here, let me show you how to be good." Through this implicit dialogue between them, the Hurrier learns how to be like the Doormat and so achieves protection from his existential terror. The satisfaction to the Doormat in this relationship derives mainly from the reassurance of security she gets from knowing that her partner's emotional dependence on their relationship is even greater than her own.

Hurrier and Try Harder

This relationship is full of tension and aggression. The Try Harder is "driven crazy" by the Hurrier, and the Hurrier is made wildly impatient by the Try Harder. Each justifies his or her own Adapted Child inadequacies in terms of the provocation of the other. The Hurrier says, "If only he weren't so damn slow, I could be calm". The Try Harder says, "If only she'd give me some peace, I could finish this". Neither of them achieves anything positive by this dishonest projection of responsibility for their hang-ups, but they may eventually succeed in provoking violence or serious bodily illness in each other.

Hurrier and Stiff Upper Lipper

This is probably the most painful relationship of all. Each of the partners is fundamentally seeking to prove the inevitability of profound loneliness, and they powerfully support each other in fulfilling this quest. The relationship often begins with the Stiff Upper Lipper acting as Rescuer of the Hurrier's Victim, but these roles are quickly succeeded by the Hurrier Persecuting and rejecting the Stiff Upper Lipper, who then becomes the Victim. The Hurrier confirms, "It's futile forming a relationship. Other people never give me what I need, so it's best to refuse what they offer me, because it won't be enough and it won't last long anyway." The Stiff Upper Lipper confirms, "No matter how much love and caring I offer another person, I am unappreciated. The only reason that makes sense is that I am intrinsically unloveworthy." The Hurrier deeply knows that her insatiable quest to be unconditionally and overwhelmingly loved is an unrealisable dream; from her all-or-nothing frame of reference, she invariably ends up with nothing. At the deepest level of his being, the Stiff Upper Lipper is so unused to receiving love that he doesn't dare form a relationship with somebody who would love him for fear that he would not know how to react. The Hurrier asks for everything and gets nothing. The Stiff Upper Lipper asks for nothing and gets nothing.

Doormat and Doormat

This couple is usually united in a very stable relationship of mutual dependence. Each of the partners is terrified of being left alone, and so they are both rigidly obedient to their unspoken agreement that they will each be and behave towards the other in accordance with conventional, respectable propriety in general, and in the ways each other ask in particular. Thus they achieve the emotional security they crave above all else. The price they pay for this is the stifling of spontaneity and authentic expression of emotion. Neither risks offending the other and so disturbing the safe equilibrium of the relationship but, to an outsider, the covert resentment between this couple is often palpable. Sometimes this relationship continues on a conventional and even keel for a lifetime; sometimes such a couple punctuates the essential politeness of the relationship with periodic angry quarrels which release (though often unconsciously) the built-up resentment each feels for his or her symbiotic dependence on the other.

Doormat and Try Harder

This is most likely to be an amicable but dreary relationship. That is, neither is likely to hurt the other, but neither will they stimulate the other to reach beyond the narrowly unambitious and respectable limits they impose on their lives. In England, it is a prototypical lower-middle-class marriage in which the wife is the Doormat and the husband the Try Harder partner. The Doormat is "nice" to the Try Harder in not pressing him to achieve anything, and the Try Harder conforms in his behaviour to the Doormat's need to be respectable. The worst they are likely to do to each other from time to time is for the Try Harder to think, but rarely say aloud, that the Doormat is affected and pretentious, and for the Doormat to think, but rarely say aloud, that the Try Harder is a failure.

Doormat and Stiff Upper Lipper

This is basically a deeply unhappy relationship, but one which often endures for a lifetime. It is very commonly the chief component of many English, and especially middle-class, marriages, the husband usually being the Stiff Upper Lipper and the wife the Doormat partner. The trouble with this relationship is that it provides each of the partners with easy affirmation of his or her most painful feelings, without providing any positive compensation. The Doormat is dependent on another's instructions as to how to behave to please the other person; the Stiff Upper Lipper longs to have his needs understood and met without his having to give voice to them. The Doormat asks the Stiff Upper Lipper to tell her what he wants her to be and to do; the Stiff Upper Lipper replies, "I want you to give to me in a spontaneous and authentic way, not according to instructions." Thus they are locked in an impasse between their incompatible needs. The Doormat accuses the Stiff Upper Lipper of being cold, and the Stiff Upper Lipper responds by crawling further and further into his shell. The Stiff Upper Lipper "proves" the impossibility of ever being loved for himself, and the Doormat "proves" she is a good person who is mis-understood and so vilified as bad.

Try Harder and Try Harder

Of all the like-to-like relationships between Adapted Child ego states, this is the one least likely to work for the benefit of both partners. (Hurrier and Hur-rier is equally unbeneficial to both partners but rarely endures for more than a few months anyhow.) At best, this couple may be united in hostility and envy towards most other people, which may, for example, find expression in their working together for a lost cause. However, it is more often the case that the envious hostility of each is projected onto the intimate other, with each chronically criticising the other in order to boost his or her own very precarious self-esteem. In this relationship, each partner will secretly sabotage the other's achievement of his or her ambitions; they are both constantly on tenterhooks lest the other win over them in some way or other. Life together for this couple is one long aggressive competition.

Try Harder and Stiff Upper Lipper

This is a relationship between essentially incompatible types. They are so fundamentally incapable of gratifying each other that a long-term relationship is unlikely between them. The Try Harder aims for what she wants materially in such a way as not to get it. The Stiff Upper Lipper asks for what he wants emotionally in such a way as not to get it. They are on different wavelengths. When this Adapted Child interaction is a minor aspect of the total relationship between a couple, the Try Harder will feel envious and aggressive towards the Stiff Upper Lipper, and the Stiff Upper Lipper will adopt a stance of cold and bored aloofness towards the Try Harder. The Try Harder envies the Stiff Upper Lipper his cool, which the Try Harder perceives herself as lacking because of insufficient luck or opportunity; and the Stiff Upper Lipper finds the Try Harder a bore for whining and generally wearing her heart on her sleeve. In transacting with each other, the Stiff Upper Lipper generally limits himself to peremptory brush-offs to the Try Harder, and the Try Harder is consumed with frustration and rage.

Stiff Upper Lipper and Stiff Upper Lipper

This relationship is characterised by a great deal of mutual independence. Each is especially averse to what they would call emotional suffocation, so they support each other in mutual understanding of the other's need for privacy. So long as both have important interests outside as well as within their relationship, they get on very well together, and they are grateful for their intimacy and commitment to each other, which relieves them of the pain they each experienced as single people reaching out for love. If one of them does not have an important interest outside the relationship, he or she will become resentful of the lack of time given to the relationship by the other; one will feel neglected, the other suffocated.

Interpersonal compounds.

Compound	Advantages	Disadvan-tages	In working relationships
Perfectionist & Perfectionist	mutual respect and harmony if values shared	mutual disharmony in judgements if values disparate	good in an equal partnership or if subordinate fully respects boss
Perfectionist & Hurrier	healthy complementarity in many areas of life	drive each other insane if either or both too great	enjoyably volatile relationship for both if Perfectionist boss; if Hurrier boss, only works if Perfectionist given lots of autonomy

(*Continued*)

Table (*Continued*).

Compound	Advantages	Disadvantages	In working relationships
Perfectionist & Doormat	Perfectionist is permitted to express wish to dominate and Doormat finds reassurance in being controlled	Perfectionist's rigidity and Doormat's inhibitions are not challenged; a narrowminded relationship	very good if Perfectionist boss; very bad if Doormat boss
Perfectionist & Try Harder	outlet for aggression of each	the chronic unhappiness of open warfare	very humiliating for Try Harder if Perfectionist boss; short-lived relationship if Try Harder boss
Perfectionist & Stiff Upper Lipper	mutual respect and intellectual pleasure	reinforce each other's a rigidity; neither's Free Child is encouraged	generally very good, "get on with it" relationship
Hurrier & Hurrier	shared futility	provoke each other into escalating self-destructiveness	very unlikely to form a relationship of any duration

(*Continued*)

Table (*Continued*).

Hurrier & Doormat	a safe harbour for Hurrier; reassur- ance of being needed for Doormat	a sense of suffocation for Hurrier; some existential insecurity for Doormat	they like each other
Hurrier & Try Harder	mutual pro- jection of responsibil- ity onto each other	Hurrier is made wildly impatient; Try Harder is "driven crazy"	open warfare
Hurrier & Stiff Upper Lipper	rationalises isolation and loneliness of each	profound unhappiness for each; only negative strokes given or received	are frightened of each other
Doormat & Doormat	emotional security for each	secret resent- ment of each towards the other; mutual inhibition of spontaneity	good mutual identification
Doormat & Try Harder	limited sta- ble security for Door- mat; some unthreatened self- esteem for Try Harder	lack of stimu- lation for either; a dull, unchanging relationship	are kind to each other

(*Continued*)

Table (*Continued*).

Compound	Advantages	Disadvan-tages	In working relationships
Doormat & Stiff Upper Lipper	may do-good together	mutual unhappiness; Doormat feels mis-understood; Stiff Upper feels unap-preciated	dislike each other
Try Harder & Try Harder	may be united in envy and hostil-ity towards others	chronic mutual aggressive competitive-ness	competitively aggressive; only good if they unite to fight "authority"
Try Harder & Stiff Upper Lipper	outlet for resentment of each	mutual hatred; Try Harder is consumed with impo-tent rage; Stiff Upper Lipper is constantly aggravated	mutual resent-ment and mis-understanding
Stiff Upper Lipper & Stiff Upper Lipper	mutual inde-pendence and respect	lack of emotional warmth or spontaneous emotional expression	generally very good; confi-dent reliance on each other

CHAPTER FIVE

Feeling

The wounded healer

What's in it for you?

It is possible to be a competent psychotherapist if you had a happy childhood and feel no significant animosity towards either of your parents, but the most potent psychotherapists are those for whom their profession is their vocation, dedicated to exorcising their own unresolved childhood pains. Parent sympathy and Adult know-how make for competence; Child empathy—which cannot effectively be dissembled—is the icing on the cake for both therapist and client.

The ultimate goal for the vocational psychotherapist is the re-telling of her own childhood story, creating with her clients an idealised version of the defective relationships she had as a child. Thus, your Child will engage with some clients through identification; with others through your projection onto them of images of the people in your childhood who most frightened, rejected, or antagonised you. While it is usually our relationships to our parents that caused us most pain, there may be other significant *dramatis personae* in our stories. In my own case, while I had an extremely painful relationship to my mother, I also felt the acute pain of Child to Child loneliness through the innate animosity between myself and my sister, my only sibling. Against the pain of our family life, we defended ourselves in opposite ways: she by determined dissociation and frivolity, I by a gloomy, desperate bid to find a companion in her to talk to about it all. Our defences were incompatible. I wasn't an only child, but I felt like one.

Thus, as a psychotherapist, especially in relationship to my groups, I have gained enormous satisfaction from finding in them brothers and sisters I never had, who have been not only willing but eager to analyse, understand, and heal the wounds that "they", our parents, imposed on us. What's it all about for you?

Therapists versus clients

Broadly speaking, therapists are inclined to be the kind of people who feel intrinsically *unloveworthy* (the Stiff Upper Lipper) and seek to *earn* love by generous giving. Broadly speaking, clients in long-term psychotherapy are inclined to be the kind of people who feel intrinsically *futile* (the Hurrier) and seek to overcome their futility by *demanding* the unconditional love they believe will give their lives meaning.

Patients and therapists are both deeply stroke-deprived, but seek remission through opposite means, which typically creates fearful antagonism between them. The usual defensive pathology in the Adapted Child of a psychotherapist is to *ask for nothing*—and so get nothing; the usual defensive pathology in the Adapted Child of a long-term patient in psychotherapy is to *ask for everything*—and so get nothing. At a deep level, such patients are frightened of the phenomenal cool self-control of the therapist; and the therapist feels unappreciated and angry in response to the greedy demands of the patient. The therapist is prompted to say to himself, "You greedy pig. If I was given even half of what I give you I would be eternally grateful." The game played out between them is one that begins with the therapist Rescuing the patient's Victim, then the patient turning Persecutor to the therapist's Victim. The therapist gets her payoff of feeling unappreciated and unloveworthy; the patient gets her payoff of triumphant, "See, I knew you wouldn't give me what I need." Most therapists are finally healed of their own deepest wounds when they have become fully resistant to this game. For a long time—perhaps years—a therapist may have to act as if she is invulnerable to such patients, but eventually the mask becomes the face.

Creativity

Boundaries and intimacy

For the traditional psychoanalyst, the tightrope act between Parent boundaries and nourishing Child to Child intimacy does not exist; boundaries are rigid and intimacy is strictly one way. His job is easy. For the rest of us, as humanistic-existential psychotherapists, we are embroiled in the creative task of finding the just-right balance between empathic self-disclosure and controlling distance. Each therapist will find her own preferred balance, which will also vary in accordance with her intuited sense of the balance that is most appropriate for particular clients.

As in all matters pertaining to being a psychotherapist, the task of finding an appropriate balance between boundaries and intimacy can be likened to the healthy relationships between parents and their children. Children, when they are at ease and secure, very much enjoy playing, in a Free Child to Free Child way, with their parents. But whenever a child is frightened or hurt or uncertain, he relies on his parents instantly and unambiguously switching into their quiet, calm, protective, controlling, reassuring Parent. And of all the nine possible ways in which a parent's Parent, Adult, and Child ego states can interact with the Parent, Adult, and Child ego states of the child, one transaction is taboo: *under no circumstances is a parent entitled to seek nourishment for her own Child from her child's Parent*. So too is the case between therapists and their clients. Overall, the most effective and ultimately most appreciated parents and psychotherapists are the ones with the most confidently expressive controlling Parent ego states.

Play

Within the boundaries of our accepted Parent responsibilities to our clients, there is nothing so invigorating between therapists and clients than exuberant, joyful play and laughter.

In my more than thirty years of being a psychotherapist, I have often felt at odds with many of my colleagues in my perception of them as being po-faced and earnest, self-righteous do-gooders. Too often, it seems to me, psychotherapists (and members of other helping professions) calibrate their effectiveness against how often and how much their clients cry; and too rarely measure their success against how often and how much they make their clients laugh. Perhaps they are defending themselves against any suspicion that they are callous in the face of human suffering, speciously believing that laughter and seriousness are incompatible. Laughter and tears are matching manifestations of deeply revelatory awareness in the Child, but laughter is much more fun.

Giving permissions

Apart from the intrinsic value of play to both therapist and client, play, coming as it does from the Free Child, offers the client permissions. Therapists coerce their clients from their Parent and offer them healing understanding from their Adult; but what they offer from their Free Child constitutes by far the greatest potential enhancement of any client's wellbeing.

Permissions effectively say, "See, I am being joyful, playful, daring, spontaneous, adventurous, risk-taking, loving, hating, happily alone … and no harm is coming to me. Here, catch!" And they do. Permissions are the opposite of (Adapted Child) inhibitions and, in particular, they are the antithesis of the fear of failure. Many people's lives are overwhelmingly constrained by their fear of failure. What if I leave my unhappy marriage and am left alone? What if I give up my hated job and can't find another? What if I confront my parents with the pain they cause me and they stop loving me? What if I start a business and lose money? What if I lose weight and put it back on again? Tell your clients about the risks you have taken in life and the rewards they have brought you, *including the inevitable failures* you have experienced on the path to success. Tell them that when they are very old, it will not be the risks they took and the failures they experienced that they will regret but only the opportunities they fearfully forsook in the name of (Adapted Child) "shoulds" and "oughts" and fears.

On the other hand, clients will see right through your hypocrisy if you try to give them permissions you yourself do not have. I remember a twenty-eight-year-old woman who, out of some deep-seated fear, was still a virgin and obsessed with her desire to lose her virginity. I cheerfully suggested that she just "do it", with more or less any man, regardless of whether she had any feeling for him. She rightfully demanded to know whether I would myself do this—which I wouldn't—and I learned a salutary lesson. Nor would I be the best therapist for somebody whose most pressing desire is to give up smoking.

Conversely, we treat best those hang-ups in our clients that we once had but have overcome, that is, where our Free Child has won out over our Adapted Child, which is the realm of our finest expertise.

And in the immediacy of our everyday therapeutic practice, if we are to be more than merely competent, it is important for us to make and be willing to display our creative mistakes, sticking our necks out in making educated best-guesses about our clients, based on the combination of our personal experience and our knowledge of human nature derived from our learned theoretical frame of reference. Never be fearful or ashamed of making mistakes in interpretation. The more willing you are sometimes to be mistaken, the more often also will you hit the nail on the head. You will also thereby be giving your clients permission sometimes to be mistaken and fail, which is the *sine qua non* of all creative achievement in all of life.

Being human

Our core myths

By and large, our myths contain two distinct, although often overlapping, themes: how we will "succeed" in the wider world, broadly based on our unfinished business with our same-sexed parent; and how we will be loved, broadly based on our unfinished business with our opposite-sexed parent.

Our unfinished business with our same-sexed parent concerns the aggrandisement of our power, which is principally focused on the achievement of status in the world at large, through what we do. Our unfinished business with our opposite-sexed parent concerns the fulfilment of our dream of being loved for what we are.

"Being" is the masculine principle in us all; being is the feminine principle in us all. So, by and large, men feel themselves unready for the fulfilment of love until their masculine self-esteem is assured through some measure of worldly accomplishment; and, by and large, women feel themselves unready wholeheartedly to pursue their careers until their feminine self-esteem is assured through loving and being loved by a man. In the long run, men need to "be" as well as "do", and women need to "do" as well as "be", in order to be wholesome human beings, and healthy intimacy, sexual or otherwise, can only flourish between two distinctly whole people.

It is in the development of spirituality associated with the quest for meaning in life that men and women can reach successfully beyond the attractions and antipathies between the sexes, to a higher level of living that encompasses masculinity and femininity and unites them in their common humanity. Broadly speaking, feeling and intuiting (the Child) is the femininity in us all, thinking and knowing-how (the Adult) is the masculinity in us all, and believing (the Parent) is the humanity in us all. But the secularisation of life has reduced morality (the Parent) to "enlightened self-interest" and left us, collectively, on the brink of despairing nihilism.

As hero or heroine of our personal myth, the process of our life is towards the triumph of fulfilment and the serenity at the end of life when, retrospectively, everything we have experienced can be seen to have been essential to our life plan, neither good nor bad, but simply the way things had to be for us.

The ideal conclusion of life is arrived at only by those who have faced and worked through the fears that stand in the way of their egos' healthily developed self-esteem, because the serene conclusion is arrived at from the vantage point that transcends the ego, and nobody has yet transcended their ego without having an ego to transcend. So, for each of us, the heroic path is becoming an ever healthier version of our own authentic self.

It is the courage and the struggle, not the outer achievement, that is the measure of a man's or woman's worth; and the private soul achievement cannot be directly known through the achievement that is visible to the world. Only in loving sexual intimacy may we learn to know another person, and ourselves be known, at the mythic centre of our beings.

Passion and pain

We are physically and psychologically bound by the limits of what we are, and it is as stupidly futile to waste our energy wishing to be psychologically other than what we are as it is to wish to be the other gender, have different-coloured eyes, or to be a different height from the one we are. But for each of us, within that unknowable amalgam of nature and nurture that made us what we are, there is a unique heroic story wanting to be told. That story was vivid to each of us in the honesty of childhood when we saw life in all its imaginative essence. Our grown-up lives are inevitably cluttered with pragmatic necessities that, if we let them, so overwhelm our consciousness that we simply plod through life as purgatory, and cynically dismiss as romantic fiction the passion and the pain and the hero-ism we have lazily renounced. We need to lift the veils of pragmatism and expediency that cloud our vision, to rediscover our dream of glory, and selfishly pursue the path to its fulfilment—to make ourselves artists and our lives the beautiful outcome of our artistry, to which satisfaction we are inherently entitled.

The heroic path is not the easy choice; it wouldn't be heroic if it were. There are dragons to be slain, and our confrontations with our personal dragons are frighten-ingly frought with the possibilities of danger and pain. Most people prefer to live myopically, disdaining and discounting the dragons and heroes and heroines in their own Child as childish. But most people who engage in psychotherapy, as practitioners or clients, aspire to a more heroic ideal in their lives than the average, pre-ferring passion, pain, and joy to the sterility of filling their lives with grown-upness and getting-by.

Revenge is sweet

The relationship between a therapist and his client is an intimate one and, notwithstanding that this intimacy is constrained by a number of special proscriptions, at a deep level, all that is true of other intimate relation-ships is also true of the therapeutic one.

While the case can be made that, deeply, we our-selves create all that we experience, phenomenally and pragmatically there is objective reality in the world and other people, which makes different people invoke different responses in us. But no relationships, happy or unhappy, occur by chance, and we are willy-nilly drawn to people who offer us the pains of our unfinished business with our parents and significant others in our formative years.

Relationships serve purposes for each of the participants and are equally mutually symbiotic for as long as they last. No relationship is ever actually "a waste" because it comes to an end, or for any other reason.

When we are in the midst of pain and loss, Adult understanding and Parent benevolence towards those who have caused us pain, without the involvement of our Child, is hypocritical; our Child must have its full say too. Blaming and hating are healthily included in the catharsis of mourning, the full pain of which is needed for the ego growth we need to make at that time. Love and hate, blame and guilt, are existentially inseparable dimensions of our passion for life at the deep irrational core of our being. People who make a proud claim to rationality in response to emotional confrontation with others are actually making a shameful admission of their inhumanity, although their repressed emotions will bitterly contaminate their outlook for the rest of their lives.

The general mythical purpose of all our intimate relationships, however unconscious we may be of it, is the fulfilment of our desire for revenge on our parents and others for the pains we experienced them as inflicting on us, especially in the eternal triangle of our Oedipal relationship to them. In our subsequent intimate relationships, we are required, by our own design, to work through our unfinished business with our parents by projectively dealing with the relevant aspects of our parents that we see in our partners, complexly mixing and matching various characteristics of both of our parents in ourselves and others. (As Saul Bellow put it so succinctly, "When a man and woman are in bed together there are at least six people in that bed.")

Having chosen a relevant intimate other, the essential meaning of the relationship will turn out to be either the pain we need at this point on our life path, readying us for joy with a different partner after we have served our appropriate sentence, or the joy of the fulfilment of our earned and achieved dream. While at the deepest level of our being, I think we prophetically know exactly what we are letting ourselves in for, being human we are all inclined consciously to the wishful thinking that causes us, at the time of entering into a relationship, to believe that this one will be the final fulfilment of our dream.

In every therapeutic encounter, the therapist as well as the client has some, however submerged, hope that this relationship will be redemptive for them.

Countertransference

While homage is paid to the feelings of the psychotherapist in the concept of countertransference, the "rights" of the client's feelings are, naturally, given priority, since he is paying freely to express his feelings, and the therapist is being paid to suppress her feelings to the extent that their expression would interfere with the client's emotional catharsis.

But therapists (like parents) are human too, and I avow the right of every therapist to draw her own lines, beyond which she will not tolerate abuse, even when only verbal.

In my own experience, there have been two occasions I can recall when I invoked my right of retaliatory emotional response, one of which got me into a lot of trouble, but was worth it for the sake of my righteousness, of which I was convinced.

The first was when a man who had recently joined a group of mine declared that he was a neo-Nazi, in response to which I screamed, "Get out—now!". Conversely, a Palestinian woman who had been in a group of mine for a few weeks, in response to my disclosure that I was Jewish, declared, with great intensity, that there was no way, therefore, that she could continue in the group. Despite my best efforts to persuade her that her and my relationship was a personal one that transcended the politics of the Middle East, she was adamant, and I regretfully accepted her point of view and her resignation.

The second occasion when I responded with my perceived right to my own humanity concerned a young man in one of my therapy groups who made a unilateral decision to leave the group while he was in the midst of a powerful negative transference onto me. He had been in the group for a couple of years and his recent intense hostility towards me was invoked by my confrontation of the smarmy inauthenticity with which he conducted his sex life. The rest of the group was unanimous in support of my best efforts to persuade this man that it would be greatly to his advantage if he were willing to work through the issues associated with his animosity towards me by continuing in his membership of the group. He refused, and the best the rest of us could do was to insist that he, not the rest of the group, was responsible for his resignation.

Seven years later, one Saturday lunchtime as I was getting out of my car in front of my home, he came up to me (to within six inches of my face) and demanded an apology of me for "ruining his life". He claimed that the negative attributions I had thrust on him had, ever since, constantly undermined his self-esteem. I listened to him respectfully and expressed my sorrow (which was genuine) that he had suffered so much. That is, I declared how sorry I was *that* he had suffered so much, although I insisted that I was not responsible for his suffering. Calmly and in my Adult—though my heart was pounding—I explained my point of view that his suffering was the price he had paid for his pre-emptive, unilateral decision to leave his therapy with me at a very critical juncture, and I offered him the option of coming to see me, on a one-to-one basis, free of charge for a couple of sessions, to work through his unfinished business with me.

With his face full of hatred, he said, "I'm never going to get an apology from you", and he turned on his heel and walked away. After he had gone a few yards, he turned round and shouted, "I hardly recognised you, you've aged so much". *I laughed—loudly*. For this, he reported me to the ethics committee of the professional association to which I belonged, which demanded of me that I repay this man all the fees he had paid me in recompense for my "abuse" of him, and that I have a number of hours of supervision to rectify my errant ways. I refused and was therefore forced to resign my membership of my professional association, which part of me experienced as a loss, but which the greater part of me considered was a welcome release from my membership of an organisation that had been corrupted by tremulous political correctness. Thankfully, this is the only unhappy encounter I have had with officialdom in my more than thirty years' experience of being a psychotherapist, but I recount it to you as a salutary warning concerning "the Child/customer is always right" ethos in which we now live.

Concerning a much lower level of distress I have experienced occasionally, I urge you to beware the seductive flattery of a client who, early on in his therapy, tells you that you are the best thing since sliced bread. Very quickly, the worm will turn. As far as possible, experience the positive as well as the negative transferences of your clients with objective detachment. Love me little, love me long.

Life and love as a game of cards

Our relationships with our clients are intimate relationships that, notwithstanding their special prescriptions and proscriptions, are essentially like all other intimate relationships we have. As in all relationships between any two people, the most fascinating considerations are the ways in which we are the same and the ways in which we are different. We are all alike in having two eyes, a nose, and a mouth ... and all uniquely different from everybody else in the infinitely various ways in which our features, both physical and psychological, are configured.

The metaphor that I find provides the most precise image of the samenesses and the differences between us is that of a pack of cards, the games that can be played with it and the hands that can be dealt. God holds the pack, which contains the totality of all that is possible; each of us is dealt a hand which is one of the virtually limitless number of possible hands. Each hand may be likened to and contrasted with any other hand in a large number of ways, the ways chosen being determined by their relevance to the game being played at any particular time.

We have no choice in the hands we are dealt; but we are free to choose which game or games we will play; and we are free to play our chosen games lightly or seriously, with desultoriness or enthusiasm, with attention or absent-mindedness, with good or bad grace, with clumsiness or artistry. No hand is intrinsically "better" or "worse" than any other; and playing out a grand slam with a fistful of court cards and trumps can be as boring as playing an adroitly skilful game with no court cards or trumps can be joyful.

Shall we only play games when our own hand grants us a head-start towards winning? Or sometimes choose to play games when the below-average value of our hand grants us the pleasure of challenging us to stretch the boundaries of our innate limitations? Shall we learn to play one game supremely well? Or enjoy the variety of learning and playing a number of games with limited skill in each? Shall we play games of high chance or high skill, for high or low stakes? In all these matters, we are free to choose and are responsible for the consequences of our choices.

Seated across the table from our partners, what must we do to make the game we are playing as pleasurable as possible for both of us? We need explicitly to establish with our partners the conventions by which we will covertly communicate to each other the contents of our respective hands; sort our cards and categorise them in a way that makes most sense within the rules of the game; make sure we have all our cards in our hand and none is hidden behind another; ascertain the strengths and weaknesses of our hand and communicate them to our partner, within the rules of the game; attend carefully to our partner's communications to us, sorting out the components of his communication into responses to us and the information he is also giving us about his own strengths and weaknesses; arrive at a mutually agreed explicit contract; play the game cooperatively, attentively, and with finesse and pleasure; apologise for any errors we make, and happily forgive our partner for his errors, with the good sportsmanship derived from our knowledge that we are both "only human" and it is "only a game".

INDEX

143